Eleanor Zuercher lives in a rural parish ⸻
(a group of six rural parishes) where s⸻
workshops for children aged 3–12 for ⸻
Eleanor oversaw all the children's wor⸻ *parish as well as being*
involved in planning and taking services until retraining as a teacher.
She now divides her time between teaching in a number of local primary
schools and working as a Deputy Registrar. Eleanor is married with a
family.

Barnabas for Children®

Barnabas for Children® is a registered word mark and the logo is a registered device mark of The Bible Reading Fellowship.

Text copyright © Eleanor Zuercher 2013
Illustrations copyright © Paula Doherty 2013,
with the exception of pp. 47, 188, 189 (copyright © Ann Kronheimer 2009)
The author asserts the moral right to be identified as the author of this work

Published by
The Bible Reading Fellowship
15 The Chambers, Vineyard
Abingdon OX14 3FE
United Kingdom
Tel: +44 (0)1865 319700
Email: enquiries@brf.org.uk
Website: www.brf.org.uk
BRF is a Registered Charity

ISBN 978 0 85746 150 6
First published 2013
10 9 8 7 6 5 4 3 2 1 0
All rights reserved

Acknowledgments
Unless otherwise stated, scripture quotations are taken from the Contemporary English Version of the Bible published by HarperCollins Publishers, copyright © 1991, 1992, 1995 American Bible Society.

Scripture quotations taken from the Holy Bible, New International Version, copyright © 1973, 1978, 1984 by International Bible Society, are used by permission of Hodder & Stoughton Publishers, a member of the Hachette Livre Group UK. All rights reserved. 'NIV' is a registered trademark of International Bible Society. UK trademark number 1448790.

Cover photographs: paper chain © Katy McDonnell/Digital Vision/Thinkstock; cake making, paints, felt pens, cup cake, hat © iStockphoto/Thinkstock; tambourine © PhotoObjects.net/Thinkstock; paintbrush © Zedcor Wholly Owned/PhotoObjects.net/Thinkstock; group of children © Hemera/Thinkstock.

The paper used in the production of this publication was supplied by mills that source their raw materials from sustainably managed forests. Soy-based inks were used in its printing and the laminate film is biodegradable.

A catalogue record for this book is available from the British Library

Printed in Singapore by Craft Print International Ltd

NOT SUNDAY, NOT SCHOOL

Bible Heroes!

A once-a-month children's programme for small churches

Eleanor Zuercher

*
This book is for some of my personal heroes:
Jenny, Jo, Chris, Heather and Michael.
You have all helped me on my way—thank you. *

Acknowledgments

Thank you, Sue, for your enthusiasm for the Not Sunday, Not School model, for editing the books and spotting my mistakes before they became an embarrassment!

My particular thanks also go to Liz, Margaret, Claire and Doll as well as the children of Acorns and Saplings, their families and especially the helpers and congregations of St Mary Magdalene in Tingewick and the rest of the West Buckingham Benefice, who allowed me to try out experimental activities on them; also, as always, Hanno, Crispin and Bertie who have to put up with me almost all the time.

Contents

How to use this book

This book contains all you need to plan through-the-year activity programmes for children, exploring stories about Bible heroes. There is material for eleven sessions based on Old Testament heroes (one for each month except August, if you wish) plus a five-day summer activity programme on New Testament heroes. Each session is designed to last approximately two hours, although this timescale can be shortened or lengthened according to need. Each session contains the following elements.

- Suggestions for Bible stories based on the theme
- Suggestions for creating a display for the church
- Craft activities
- Games
- Suggestions for prayer

Timing

Each activity is designed to last between 5 and 20 minutes, and the ideas are intended to be used on a pick-and-mix basis to help you create your own programme. Sample plans for each session, showing an outline programme, can be found on the website www.barnabasinchurches.org.uk/extra-resources/. A sample plan for the story of Abraham is also shown on page 178 of this book (Appendix 1).

Since so much depends on the age, interests and abilities of the children, you may find that activities will take longer or much less time. Therefore, the timings given in the sample plans are guidelines only. Activities could also be run simultaneously, so that the children move in groups from one activity to the next if time and space round the tables is short.

The suggested activities for creating a display for the church are designed to last between 15 and 20 minutes. However, depending on the age and ability of the children, more time can be spent on them if required.

Additional material

Visit the Barnabas website, www.barnabasinchurches.org.uk/extra-resources/, for additional material, such as extra ideas for integrating children's work into the wider congregation (especially important if your children meet at a time other than Sunday morning). Additional materials can be downloaded free of charge.

Introduction

Although we tend to focus (quite understandably) on Jesus and Gospel stories when teaching children in Sunday schools and church clubs, Old Testament stories also deserve some airing. As children encounter fewer Bible stories in schools and at home than they did in the past, many Old Testament stories will be unfamiliar and fresh for children who have not heard them before. Many are action-packed and exciting and will appeal widely to children who are used to fast-paced films or television and computer or console games.

Some children can lose interest in stories that don't include a lot of dramatic action and, while there is plenty of drama in many Old Testament stories, you will need to consider how to present some parts of them in an appropriate way. If you are re-reading them for the first time since childhood, you may be surprised at some of the content. Old Testament stories can point the way to Jesus, and there are questions for children in each chapter of this book to help them think about the connection between the Old Testament and Jesus. In addition, the final chapters enter the New Testament to give a sense of the journey from old to new and fulfilment in Jesus.

Alongside reasons of faith development, there are important cultural reasons for hearing Old Testament stories: much of our culture's literature and music from a less secular (and quite recent) past makes frequent biblical reference.

Some obvious Bible heroes, such as Noah, Moses, and Jonah, are omitted from this book because materials on them have already been published in *Not Sunday, Not School!* and *Bible Journeys Holiday Club*, both of which are available from the Barnabas website, www.barnabasinchurches.org.uk.

The rural context

The material in *Not Sunday, Not School Bible Heroes!* is based on the experience of working with children in a rural context. However, many of the principles applied to the rural setting are equally relevant to an urban, suburban or larger town situation. Due to low numbers and the dispersion of the community, children's work in small rural communities can be immensely challenging and it is often not possible to presuppose that the work can follow the traditional model of meeting each week on Sunday morning while the adults attend the morning service. Therefore, it is paramount to consider a range of concerns, which may, of course, also apply to non-rural situations. These include the following considerations.

- The best day and time for your children's work.
- The best place to hold your meetings.
- The best mixture of activities.
- Who will be responsible for which tasks.
- How to advertise your club.
- How to identify suitable sources of funding.
- How to ensure that all child protection and health and safety measures are in place.
- What to do about potential difficulties, such as lack of toilets or kitchen facilities.

Opportunities and advantages

The challenge of working with a small number of children also provides an ideal opportunity for encouragement and reward. For example, small numbers mean that you will be able to get to know and serve individual children far better. Also, you have the advantage of being able to tailor your children's work to your own individual requirements.

Don't worry if you don't have a limitless expenses fund and all the state-of-the-art technology on the market. Concentrate instead on making your programmes imaginative, creative and unique. The enjoyment the children get out of your sessions will not depend on technology; that is only a means to an end. Also, if you are lacking a nicely furnished, carpeted, warm room, make sure you use the symbolism, images and atmosphere available in the building you do use—especially if it is the church. The church building is entirely different from any other the children are likely to enter on a regular basis. They will appreciate that it is special, particularly if you make their time there special too.

Don't worry if you are unable to run a children's church alongside the main service on a Sunday morning. It is far better practice and richer in spiritual terms if the children are welcomed as part of the normal pattern of worship along with adult members of the congregation. Having the children present will also help adults and children to learn from each other in their understanding of faith and the Bible, so encourage your church leadership to ensure that provision is made to include children fully in Sunday worship.

Use your session times productively by keeping the teaching focused. Rather than coming to church on a regular basis, some children may only attend the monthly club, so this will be a golden opportunity for them to hear the basic Christian stories, perhaps for the first time.

Planning and preparation

As you would expect, if children's work is to be successful it needs careful planning and preparation. Some of the activities in this book require more preparation than others, but time spent in this area is always worthwhile. Make sure you give the children good-quality resources to use. It is a good idea to try out the ideas at home first, so that you know how they work and can show the children a finished example.

Alongside the workshop ideas, you may wish to add songs or percussion music to your programme. As well as using your own style of music and favourite songs, it is a good idea to find out what songs the children sing at school and use this information to enlarge your repertoire.

You will also need to give some consideration to the presentation of the stories about the Bible heroes. This can be varied from programme to programme by using different storytelling methods. For example, you could use a child-friendly Bible translation, such as the Contemporary English Version, or a children's storytelling Bible, such as *The Barnabas Children's Bible* (Barnabas, 2007). Alternatively, you could tell the story using visual aids, actions, mime or drama.

There are some interactive stories in this book, together with some biblical guided meditations which encourage audience participation in some form. Old Testament stories in particular are often quite long or spread intermittently over several chapters in the Bible, so a paraphrase can help when presenting the stories to children.

The guided visualisations in this book help children to imagine or pray their way into the story. When using these visualisations, make sure the children are sitting comfortably. The words should be read quietly, leaving plenty of pauses for imaginations to work. It may take a few attempts for the children to get used to the technique, but it is worth persevering.

Integrating children's work within the church and community

One of the problems that may arise if your children's work does not operate on a Sunday morning is that the adult congregation may forget, or be unaware of, what is available for children. The ideas below should ensure that the profile is kept high and that everyone is encouraged to pray for the children's activities.

Identity

Choose a suitable name for your group and display it prominently in the church building. For example, you could make a simple banner with the name painted on it and children's handprints to decorate it. Also, make sure there are articles and advertisements in your church magazine, using your group name.

Children's council

Having a link between the children and the church council (or your equivalent) is a very useful way to ensure that your church leaders are informed about the children's work. This can also serve as a valuable way of setting up communication links, but make sure that it is two-way communication. You might want to consider having your children's leader or a representative specifically for children and young people on the church council.

To make the communication process easier, you might consider setting up a children's council. Many schools have children's councils, so children are often used to being asked for and articulating their views. If children's opinions are sought and respected in schools and other contexts, churches need to make sure children are also given a voice in the church setting. A children's church council will give them a chance to air their views, with regard to their own activities and to the life of their church as a whole. Adult members of the congregation may learn more about the spiritual maturity of children in their midst from this process than they might anticipate.

Worship

If the children's activities are run outside normal service times, there is a danger that all-age worship may be put slightly lower on the list of priorities. To remedy this, and to remind the rest of the worshipping community about the children, it is important to ensure that children and their families can be welcomed at any service. Families need to have the opportunity to worship together, as well as provision being made for children to learn about faith with suitable activities and stories. For example, alongside the mainstream services, you may wish to find ways for the children to make a special contribution for the celebration of a major festival.

Local links

Local organisations, of which your church is one, can provide useful links. For example, your local school might find the resource of your church building very useful, not only for the provision of the RE curriculum but also for holding large festival assemblies, attended by parents as well as children. Schools often invite professional people to take assemblies, and children's work leaders are likely candidates for an invitation. An added bonus to visiting the school is that pupils will get to know you and what you do. Word of mouth spreads quickly, and more children may be interested in coming to church-based activities and events. Also, the local school may be a willing source for items such as harvest gifts or displays to decorate the church.

Other organisations or clubs might be able to contribute specialist themes. For example, a flower arranger could help the children to create special church decorations or something for Mothering Sunday; someone from the historical society could talk to the children about the locality; a local artist could demonstrate different media, and so on.

Longer-term projects

The children may enjoy being involved in slightly longer-term projects, such as producing their own version of the church guide. You could use the celebration of Pentecost as a starting point. Think about how the church is the people rather than the building, and invite the children to write and draw pictures about how different people contribute. Don't leave out the fascinating information about the building, but present it in a way that interests and involves the children. You could include a plan of the church and a treasure hunt, which sends them round the building looking for historical clues. A photograph of a stained-glass window could be traced to produce a colouring page for younger children. Include children's pictures and ideas mixed with photographs, and adult-produced maps and puzzles.

If you have any keen needleworkers, you could organise a design-a-kneeler project. If your church already has modern handmade kneelers and you know of a supplier, you simply need to measure your existing kneelers. If this is not the case, suppliers can be found via the internet or through church journals. The children draw their design on a piece of A3 paper, using bold shapes and bright colours. Members of the adult congregation can then get involved by either stitching the designs or sponsoring the materials needed to make up the kneelers. The number of designs needed will depend on the number of stitchers and sponsors.

You can buy blank kneeler kits from suppliers and, using a squared grid, you will be able to work out how much of each coloured thread you will need to complete each design (not forgetting the sides, of course). You may need to adapt colours slightly for financial and aesthetic reasons. Transferring the design itself is easy: by placing the picture (or a copy of it) underneath the canvas, the design can be drawn on using felt-tip pen. After a few weeks' work, you will have a series of colourful, original and highly unusual kneelers for your church. It's a nice idea to stitch the designer's name and age on the side of the kneeler for posterity. Fuller instructions for this activity can be found on the website, www.barnabasinchurches.org.uk/nsns. (Click on 'Download the additional material'.)

As an alternative to stitched kneelers, you may wish to consider working together to produce some banners for the church. You will need to plan how many designs are to be incorporated and how they are to be arranged, as well as how they will be connected, whether by directly stitching one to the next or by stitching borders in between to frame each piece. The longevity and general finish of the whole project will also be improved by attaching a lining to the back. As the designs will be displayed together, it might also be appropriate to plan the finished piece around a theme—perhaps the life of your patronal saint or a biblical theme. When all the pieces are finished, you could organise a social stitching event to join everything together, unless it is easier for one person to take charge to produce the finished product.

Child protection and health and safety

It is essential that you give both child protection and health and safety considerable attention. Your diocese (or equivalent) should be able to provide you with detailed information about what is required and how to go about fulfilling the requirements. You must follow your diocese's guidelines. It is vitally important that all your helpers have Criminal Records Bureau (CRB) criminal record checks (visit the website www.homeoffice.gov.uk/agencies-public-bodies/crb for more information) and that you comply with the law by making sure that you run your sessions with proper attention to child protection and health and safety. Remember that the safeguards are there to protect not only the children who are in your care but also the adult helpers. Where you need assistance, ask for help. Obtaining clearance and holding records can easily be done by someone who wishes to support your children's work but may not be able to offer any physical help.

Child protection

Make sure you know how a child's disclosure of neglect or abuse at home should be handled. Check this with your diocese or equivalent. You should find that there is someone nominated by the diocese to deal with these issues, which will avoid the situation (particularly destructive in close-knit communities) of neighbours being told, or perhaps the minister becoming aware of too much detail, which could make it difficult for him or her to continue to support the whole family. You may think that this scenario is unlikely in a small community where everyone appears to know everyone else's business, but we can never be sure what goes on behind closed doors. Waiting until after the disclosure has been made before finding out how it should have been handled is too late.

Check the requirements for the ratio of adults to children at your sessions. This will depend on the age of the children present, but you should always have enough adults to ensure that there are at least two present at any time with any child. Allow for the possibility of one adult having to leave the room for some reason: there should always be two left behind.

First aid

At least one adult in each session should be a qualified first aider. If you need more people to be qualified, find out about local training courses for child first aid.

Registration

Make sure you have documentation giving information about the children in your care. A simple registration form will suffice. It should give the name and date of birth of the child, contact details including emergency contact details, information about any allergies and the name of the child's doctor. Permissions for things like administration of first aid and taking of photographs should also be included.

A signing in and signing out form for parents as they drop and collect children will ensure that you know which children are present at any time. You will need to know exactly how and when this form will be completed so that it is always accurate. The form should include space for parents to notify you if someone else will be collecting their children.

Sample forms for registration, parental consent and signing in and out can be found on the website www.barnabasinchurches. org.uk/nsns/.

Health and safety

Carry out a risk assessment by viewing the building or room(s) you will be using from a child's point of view. Take particular note of doors that may need to be watched to ensure that children don't escape during the session.

If you are using an ancient church building, be aware of steep stone steps, unguarded heaters, things that are shouting out to be climbed, or other hazards. Such hazards may not preclude the use of the building, but some will need to be dealt with, for example, by placing secure guards around heaters and designating certain areas as out-of-bounds. No room can ever be completely safe, but you must take every precaution to safeguard the children in your care.

Make sure that the electrical checks on wiring and equipment, and the fire extinguisher checks, are all up to date and that you have appropriate insurance cover. Check this with your PCC or governing council if you are unsure.

Finally, make sure you know where the fire exits are, and that they are accessible in the event of fire.

The story of Abraham

Key Bible focus

Leave your country, your family, and your relatives and go to the land that I will show you. I will bless you and make your descendants into a great nation. You will become famous and be a blessing to others.

GENESIS 12:1–2

In the story of Abraham, we learn about his unquestioning obedience and trust in God and discover that history might have been very different if it hadn't been for Abraham's faith. In recognition of his obedience, God made promises to Abraham about his son in particular and his descendants in general on quite a few occasions. In your exploration of the story of Abraham with children, you might want to think about how God promised to reward Abraham for his obedience. The difficult story of the near-sacrifice of Isaac demonstrates the lengths to which Abraham was prepared to take that obedience.

We can learn that God does reward obedience, although perhaps it is not always an immediate reward.

Read the story of Abraham from a children's Bible or Bible storybook.

- What other Bible stories involve people obeying God? Were they rewarded? (Jesus provides the ultimate example of obedience to God's will. What was his reward? Sometimes the reward isn't one that we can understand or perceive.)
- What other Bible stories involve someone sacrificing their own son?

Displays for the church

Fingerpaint a crowd

This display reflects the idea of Abraham's descendants being so numerous. Whether or not we are his actual descendants, all believers are his spiritual descendants.

> You will need: a large sheet of paper (size will depend on the number of children but lining paper or plain wallpaper cut from a roll would work for larger groups, or A1 sugar paper for smaller ones); paints; felt-tip pens; hand-washing equipment.

Make it

Invite the children to create a crowd scene by dabbing fingerprints on to the paper to make the faces of the crowd. (To speed things up, they can print up to five faces at a time per hand.) When the paint is dry, use the felt-tip pens to draw features on to the faces. Perhaps children could start by making a face for every person they can think of.

You could finish the frieze by adding the words, 'I will bless you and make your descendants into a great nation.'

Chat about it

Talk about what it means to be a descendant of Abraham. In what sense are we his descendants? Who else is a spiritual descendant? (You might want to go into the question of Judaism and Islam, which, in this sense, also 'descend' from Abraham.)

Trinity icon

There are several iconic depictions of Abraham's three visitors (find the story in Genesis 18:1–15). Have a look at some pictures and talk about what they show. You should be able to download suitable images from the internet. If you have a small group, you might wish to create a tableau of the scene.

Alternatively, you could make a large collage icon of the same scene. Sketch the outline of the scene on a large piece of card mounted on a solid board. Then supply glue and collage materials, such as fabrics, tissue, different papers and so on, and invite the children to complete each section in collage. If you are doing this in the style of an icon, make sure you have plenty of gold paper and rich colours.

Chat about it

Talk about how we might recognise an angel or even God himself. How do we know when God is asking us to obey him?

Craft activities

Trinity spinners

Because the visit of the three men to Abraham is sometimes interpreted by Christians as a representation of the Trinity, you could make spinners to demonstrate how three colours can become one.

> You will need: white card; compasses; cocktail sticks; Plasticine®; colouring pens or pencils.

Make it

Mark circles of card using the compasses and cut them out. Mark the circles into three roughly equal segments. Give each child a circle and invite them to colour each of the three segments a different colour. Push a cocktail stick through the hole in the centre and use a small piece of Plasticine® both to keep the stick in the right place and to give a bit of weight to the top, to balance it. Spin the top and watch what happens to the colours: three become one.

Sand pictures

You will need: card (thick enough to take glue and sand); different coloured sands or grit (available from aquarium shops); PVA glue; string (optional).

Make it

Show the children the different coloured sands or grit and demonstrate how to spread glue on the card, sprinkle the sand on top and shake off any excess (exactly like glitter). Invite the children to create their own pictures using this technique and the different coloured sands. If the children want clear definition between areas of colour, use the string to mark out the picture and fill in the various areas. You could try making colours you lack by mixing different sands together.

Chat about it

Talk about God's promise to Abraham about his descendants. How many might there be? Just like the sand, we're all different colours, too.

Flicking stars into space

You will need: pictures of the Milky Way; black paper; white or silver paint (you could use other pastel shades too); toothbrushes; paint; hand-washing equipment; plastic sheeting to protect the surrounding area.

Make it

You will probably need to practise first with some paper and paint to judge the right consistency for the paint. Show the children pictures of the Milky Way and talk about the huge number of stars and planets it contains. Show the children how you can load a toothbrush with paint and then, by drawing your thumb across the brush, splatter the paint on to the paper. (Make sure you move your thumb towards yourself.) Invite the children to take turns to create their own galaxies.

Chat about it

There is plenty of scope here to talk about the number of stars. If you are using coloured paint, you could also talk about how stars have different colours when viewed through a telescope, depending on how hot they are. You might also show the children some colour images from the Hubble space telescope.

Cooking

Angel cakes

You will need:

- 2 eggs
- 115g sugar
- 115g butter
- 115g self-raising flour
- pinch of salt
- flavouring such as vanilla extract or lemon zest if required.

You will also need: mixing bowls; mixing spoons; paper cake cases; scales; hand-washing equipment; icing ingredients (icing sugar and water or lemon juice); edible sprinkles.

Make it

First, make sure everyone has washed and dried their hands properly. Make the cake mixture by creaming together the butter and sugar until they are light and fluffy. Add the eggs one at a time, mixing well between each, add any flavouring you are using, then fold in the flour. Put about one and a half teaspoons of mixture into each paper cake case (if you are using muffin cake cases, you will need to use more). Bake in the oven at about 180°C/Gas 4 for around ten minutes. This quantity should make about 16 small cakes.

If this seems like too much effort and mess, you could always buy some ready-made plain cupcakes and ice them.

For the icing, wait until the cakes are cold (or use bought ones). Mix the icing sugar with a little water or lemon juice (which takes the extreme sweetness off the icing) to a smooth but not too watery consistency. Invite the children to dribble icing, using teaspoons, over the cakes. If you're feeling adventurous, you could use different colours to get some interesting effects. Finish with a generous helping of edible sprinkles.

Chat about it

How did Abraham feed his guests? What might you give to an angel who came for tea? How would you know if one did?

Think of other times in the Bible when angels or even God came to visit someone, perhaps sharing food with them.

Games

Truth or lie

Abraham believed in God's promises, but it's not always easy to know what to believe.

There are two ways to play the truth or lie game. The first method is to write a series of amazing facts on envelopes. Inside each envelope, insert a card indicating whether the fact is true or false. As the children take turns to read each fact, the others guess whether it is true or not.

Alternatively, organise the children into two teams. Give each team an amazing fact and ask them to make up another two false statements to go with it. The opposing team has to guess which of the three statements is true. This version of the game requires the children to be mature enough to be able to write some bluff statements that have a ring of truth about them.

Auction of promises

If you need an idea for fund-raising, you could launch an auction of promises on the back of this session. If parents have had lots of involvement in the session, it might be something that they could organise for themselves. Be aware that if you want to use this as an opportunity for the children to raise money, there are safety implications: you need to think about what is being promised and who is buying the promises. For this reason, it may be better to organise a group promise such as litter-picking or weeding in a safe environment, or car washing or a shoe-shine service, so that the promise can be performed as a group with supervision.

Prayers

Sandy prayers

Provide a large tray of dry sand. As prayers are said, invite the children to allow a handful of sand to trickle through their fingers. You will need to make sure the children are in a quiet, reflective mood, or risk the over-excitement brought on by sandpits!

This session might present a good opportunity to thank God for our community of faith, deriving from our descent from Abraham, and to remember those who walk with us or have gone ahead. You might want to ask for help to bridge the gaps between denominations or faiths.

Candle prayers

Give each child a candle and light them. (Do this only if the children are old enough to handle a candle responsibly. Alternatively, light a group of candles on a table out of reach as a prayer focus.) Think about the symbolism of Jesus as the light for the world and ask for grace to recognise God or his message when it presents itself even if we are busy, or if it comes in an unexpected form. Ask for grace to obey when we hear God's call.

Guided visualisation on stars

God promised Abraham that his descendants would be as numerous as the stars. Read the text below softly, allowing plenty of pauses for the children's imaginations to work. You will need to adapt the sounds that children might hear, at the beginning and end of the visualisation, to your particular environment.

Invite everyone to sit comfortably—back straight, shoulders relaxed, feet on the floor—and close their eyes. The children may take a little while to settle, and it may take a few attempts at this sort of activity for them to get the hang of stillness.

Listen to the sounds you can hear around you. Focus first on the sounds you can hear that are far away. What is the faintest sound? An aeroplane flying overhead? The wind in the trees outside? Birds singing?

Listen to the sounds from other parts of the building—perhaps conversations happening in another room. Now try to hear sounds within the room—the hum of the lights, the tick as the hands on the clock move round, the sound of my voice and of people sitting nearby shifting slightly.

Now listen to the sounds within yourself—the thump of your heart, breath filling and emptying from your lungs, blood rushing through the veins in your ears.

Imagine a perfect, beautiful, warm summer evening after a blissful day spent in the most beautiful countryside. You are lying outside. It is comfortable and you feel completely safe and relaxed. You gaze up at the sky as night begins to fall.

Watch the colours of the sky as the golden sun slowly turns to orange, then a burning red as it sinks beneath the horizon. The pale blue sky in the west slowly darkens, through all the shades of blue you can imagine to inky midnight blue, as you gaze upwards. You feel the warm breeze on your face; you feel at home here. This is your place in the universe.

Watch as the stars begin to appear, gradually at first as the sky continues to darken, then more and more thickly as the sky begins to look like the inside of a huge dome dotted with bright points of light—so many that you couldn't possibly count them. You can see the glow of the stars in the Milky Way spread out over your head, sweeping across the sky. Enjoy the beauty of the sky, its majesty and grandeur.

As you watch the stars, you realise that you are not just seeing black sky and white light. Each star has a different sort of light, almost like a colour, some tinged with red, others yellow or even blue. You realise that they do not stay in the same places but seem to be moving across the sky, making patterns.

Imagine you can listen to the stars. What might they sound like? Might they speak or sing? What sounds might they make? How could they sound all together?

Think about how far away they are. How long have they been shining? When did the light that you see today leave each star? Marvel at the vastness of the universe, the variety, the diversity. Take time to wonder at it. This is your home, where you belong.

Although the stars seem to be moving slowly, you can imagine that at such a distance they are whirling and dancing at a joyous pace all through the heavens. You realise that you too are part of the dance. The earth is part of the pattern they make through space and you are part of the earth. Take a moment to enjoy the dance… to hear the sound of it, to relish the joy of it, to take hold of it, own it and be part of it. Become one with it.

Now we need to return to that perfect spot, lying beneath the heavens, gazing at the starry night sky, feeling the warmth of the breeze and the comfort of the ground. Watch as the sky begins to pale and the stars fade against the brightening sky of another day. As you lie there, listen to the sound of the blood in your ears… air filling and emptying from your lungs… your heart thumping. As you allow yourself to come back into our room, begin to listen to the sounds in the room, the hum of the lights, the tick of the clock, the sound of my voice. Now listen to sounds outside and the furthest sound you can possibly hear.

When you're ready, have a good stretch and open your eyes.

— Theme 2 —

The story of Joseph

Key Bible focus

Joseph's brothers said to each other, 'What if Joseph still hates us and wants to get even with us for all the cruel things we did to him?' ... But Joseph told them, 'Don't be afraid! I have no right to change what God has decided. You tried to harm me, but God made it turn out for the best, so that he could save all these people, as he is now doing. Don't be afraid! I will take care of you and your children.' After Joseph said this, his brothers felt much better.

GENESIS 50:15, 19–21

The story of Joseph is popular and may well be familiar to the children, particularly if they have seen or heard of the musical version. The story is long, with many events that you might choose to highlight. Perhaps you could focus on the theme of brotherly love, forgiveness even of those who have tried to do us harm, and trust in God.

The story of Joseph is spread out between Genesis 37 and 50, so it will need some abridgment if you are reading it from a Bible. To do it justice, you might want to spread the telling over a number of sessions. You could tell the stories using video extracts, perhaps even using the musical, or you could use your own words or a children's Bible or picture book.

The stories include Joseph being sold into slavery (Genesis 37:12–36), Joseph in Egypt (Genesis 39—41), and Joseph meeting his brothers again (Genesis 42—45).

When you have told the story or stories, discuss them with the children.

- After all he had gone through, Joseph was still prepared to forgive the brothers who had tried to do him such harm. Can you think of anyone else in the Bible who was prepared to forgive those who tried to harm him?

Displays for the church

Coat of many colours

You will need: a 'coat' to decorate (an old white lab coat would be excellent for this purpose); strips of coloured fabric or ribbons; glitter glue; sequins; glue.

Make it

Invite the children to glue fabric strips or patches on to the coat to make it multicoloured. Add some extra glittery decoration using sequins and glitter glue. Allow the glue to dry and display the garment on a coathanger or, if you have one, a dressmaker's dummy.

Chat about it

Talk about what Joseph's coat might have looked like. How did Joseph feel when he wore it? How did his brothers feel about it? How do beautiful new clothes make you feel?

Craft activities

Corn and stars printing

You will need: black card or thick paper; gold and silver acrylic paint; potatoes cut with a star pattern (use a star-shaped biscuit cutter and then trim with a knife for a good shape); string glued round a rolling-pin.

Make it

Apply paint, sparingly, to the potato and the rolling-pin, using a brush. Then print on to the black paper, using the rolling-pin to make corn stalks and fingerprints for the grains of wheat, set alongside one another to make ears of wheat. Print with the prepared potatoes to add stars to the paper.

Chat about it

Discuss Joseph's dreams with the children. How did his brothers feel about Joseph's dream? If you had had those dreams, what would you have thought about them?

Prison bar pictures

You will need: white paper; strips of black card; drawing and colouring materials.

Make it

Talk about what Joseph might have seen out of his prison window, or perhaps what place he might have been thinking about when he was in prison. Invite the children to draw and colour a picture of the world outside, or the world in Joseph's imagination, and then stick the black card strips over their picture as prison bars.

Chat about it

How might Joseph have felt, being in prison in a foreign place?

Family trees

Sensitivity may be required for this activity, particularly in respect of children from broken homes. It is also time-consuming, but, if you have a small group of children whom you know well, you might find it useful.

You will need: A3 sheets of paper; paper slips with Joseph's family's names written on them; blank paper slips; pens; glue.

Make it

Talk to the children about who Joseph's family were and how they were all related to one another. Explain how a family tree works and how to construct one.

Use the prepared slips of paper to create Joseph's family tree. Then invite the children to write the names of people in their families and/or draw pictures of them on separate slips of paper. Help children to construct their own family trees (younger ones could just include parents, siblings and cousins).

Using slips of paper enables names to be moved around until they are in the right place, before gluing them on and drawing the connecting lines.

Chat about it

What does it mean to be in a family? How do families fit together? What expectations do we have of our families?

Dream catchers

You will need: basket-making wicker; ribbons; string or wool; beads, sequins and so on.

Make it

Use the basket-making wicker to construct hoops for the dream catchers (older children could make their own). Show the children how to wind the string or wool across the frame, stringing beads on to it as you go. Finish by threading some colourful ribbon through the string net. Help the children with their own creations. The dream catchers can be hung from the ceiling for display.

As a variation, you could make an extra-large dream catcher as a display item for your church.

Chat about it

What do you think about dreams? Do you remember dreams? Is it possible to catch them?

3D star dreams

> You will need: 3D star shapes (see template in Appendix 3) in pairs, with slits, cut from white card; pens.

Make it

Show the children how the pairs of star shapes fit together. Invite them to decorate their stars with dream pictures—their own or Joseph's.

Chat about it

Can you remember your dreams? What do you like to dream about?

Treasure boxes

> You will need: plain small boxes with lids; glue; sequins; beads; jewels.

Make it

Invite the children to decorate their boxes to make them look as special as possible—as if they might contain treasure. Remind them that the lids need to be removable, so they must be careful with the glue!

Chat about it

Discuss how Joseph became rich in Egypt. How was it different from his previous life? Did he enjoy his wealth and status? What might he have missed? Can you think of anyone else in the Bible who gave up status (and riches of a non-earthly type) to become poor?

Photo frames

You will need to take a group photograph at the beginning of the session and arrange to have it printed several times for this activity.

> You will need: a digital camera and the ability to print photos quickly; printed photographs; photo mounts; pens; masking tape.

Make it

Talk about how Joseph's family might have celebrated finding Joseph again. If they had had cameras, they might have taken photographs as part of the occasion, as we do at events like weddings, to help us remember them.

Show the children the group photograph taken at the beginning of the session. Invite them to decorate a photo mount each. When their mounts are finished, give them a copy of the photo and help them to fix it using masking tape at the back.

Chat about it

How might Joseph's family have felt about finding one another again? How did they feel about selling Joseph at the beginning of the story? Can you think of any other Bible stories about the lost being found?

Sealing wax

The 'seals' will need to be made in advance. Find some decorative buttons, such as the metal sort with anchors or shields embossed on to them. These need to be fixed securely (try using a glue gun) to a cork or something similar so that they can be used for sealing without the risk of burnt fingers. This activity is more suited to older children.

> You will need: sealing wax; parchment paper; buttons mounted securely on corks; ribbon; candle and matches.

Make it

Show the children pictures of sealed documents, or an original sealed document if you have one, and explain how seals were used in the past. Demonstrate how to use sealing wax to make a seal—melting the wax in the candle flame, applying it to the paper and then quickly making an impression in the wax with the button seal.

Encourage children to make their own official document and then apply a seal (or seals). If they want to seal a piece of ribbon underneath, they could do so.

Great care will need to be taken with the candle flame and the molten sealing wax. Have a bucket of sand standing by, in case of need. You may think it better to put dollops of wax on the paper yourself and just allow the children to make the seal impression.

Chat about it

Why was entrusting a seal to Joseph such an important action? What did it enable Joseph to do?

Cooking

Star biscuits

> You will need: biscuit dough (see Appendix 2 for a recipe); rolling-pins; baking parchment; baking trays; biscuit cutters; work surface; hand-washing equipment.

Make it

Give each child some biscuit dough and show them how to roll the dough out to about half a centimetre thick and cut out star shapes. Invite the children to place their biscuit stars on named pieces of baking parchment, ready for baking.

If you don't have facilities for baking in your venue, have slips of paper ready with baking instructions so that the children can bake their biscuits at home.

Bird pudding

NB: this is not for human consumption.

> You will need: solid cooking fat; breadcrumbs; oats; cooked potato; yoghurt pots; string; bowl and pan; hot water; Plasticine®.

Make it

Make a hole in the bottom of a pot and thread the string through, tying a knot in the end inside the pot. Seal the outside with a small piece of Plasticine®.

Then, make the bird pudding. Melt the cooking fat using a bowl placed over a pan of hot water. Invite the children to add the breadcrumbs, oats and cooked potato to the fat and mix it well. Pour the mixture into the pots and leave it to harden.

The pots of bird pudding can be hung upside down in the garden to attract birds when food is hard for them to find.

Chat about it

Why might hungry birds be an indication of a difficult time for humans?

Games

Hunt the cup

You will need: small laminated pictures to be hidden around your venue (lots of pictures of different types of treasure, but just one of them must be a picture of a cup).

Play it

Invite the children to hunt the treasure, but tell them that they're looking for the cup in particular.

Chat about it

Can you think of any other Bible stories about looking for treasure?

Memory game

You will need: pairs of laminated picture cards showing different types of treasure. One pair must be pictures of a cup (but you should hide one of the cup pictures somewhere in your room, so that you have an odd number of cards left).

Play it

Lay out the cards randomly, so that the children can't tell that there is an odd number. Children take turns to turn over two cards at a time. If they turn over a pair, they can keep the cards and have another go. If the cards don't match, they must turn the cards upside down again. Continue until all the pairs have been taken.

What's left? Ask children to look around the room for the missing cup picture.

Prayers

Star prayers

Hand out some star shapes (you could use star-shaped sticky notes) and invite the children to write or draw their prayers on the shapes. Invite them to stick their stars to a black sheet of card as prayers are said.

You might consider focusing prayers at the end of the session particularly on our families. Pray that we will always be prepared to share our good fortune with others.

Wheat prayers

If it is the right time of year, children could add a stalk of wheat to a vase to represent their prayers. If the season is not right, each child could add a card shaped like a grain of wheat, to make a whole large ear of wheat, to represent prayers.

Wheat prayers might be appropriate to thank God for giving us enough to eat and drink, and to pray for people who lack these things.

The story of Gideon

Key Bible focus

Gideon prayed to God again. 'Don't be angry at me,' Gideon said. 'Let me try this just one more time, so I'll really be sure you'll help me. Only this time, let the wool be dry and the stone floor be wet with dew.' That night, God made the stone floor wet with dew, but he kept the wool dry.

JUDGES 6:39–40

This story of a battle and a victory against all odds, led by a man who is surprised to be a leader, has a lot to offer.

The story of Gideon is found in Judges 6—8. It can be told in an interactive way in two halves. The first deals with God's communications with Gideon, which could incorporate and flow into the 'Wet wool experiment' discussion idea below.

The second half relates to the use of trumpets and lamps. This story might be used at the end of the session, with opportunities for the children (at the appropriate moments) to toot their trumpets and light their lamps.

Read the story of Gideon from a children's Bible or Bible storybook.

- Although Gideon's faith was a bit shaky to begin with, in the end he trusted God so much that he was prepared to let most of his warriors go home, knowing that, despite the overwhelming odds, God would fulfil his promises. Can you think of anyone else in the Bible who trusted God to fulfil his promises despite overwhelming odds?

Displays for the church

Flowerpot lamps

You will need: terracotta flowerpots painted with white emulsion; acrylic paint; paintbrushes; tealights or votive candles; extra-long matches or tapers.

Make it

Pre-painting the flowerpots with white emulsion will give a good surface on which to apply the acrylic paint and will improve the brightness of the colours the children use.

Give each child a prepared flowerpot and invite them to decorate their pot with acrylic paint: they could paint Gideon's battle, or sheep, or an abstract pattern. When the pots are dry, hand out tealights or votive candles to put in each pot. You will need extra-long matches or tapers, especially if you use tealights, to light the candles safely.

Chat about it

How might lamps have helped Gideon win a battle? What was the most important advantage Gideon had?

Craft activities

Wool-winding pictures

You will need: mounting board cut into rectangles (about 10cm × 15cm is fine, but include some variety); wool in a variety of colours and textures; double-sided tape.

Make it

Stick double-sided tape down opposite sides of the rectangles on what will be the back of the picture. The children make their pictures by winding wool round the mounting board so that the strands are close together and the board cannot be seen in between. Change colours and textures of wool when desired.

Children could make abstract designs or a landscape, such as a desert scene, in which case they will need to think about proportions of sky and land (approximately two-thirds sky to one-third land will look best).

The card can be used landscape or portrait. The wool will stick on the double-sided tape to be held securely.

Wool craft

If you have helpers who can knit or crochet, you might introduce this craft to the children. You could also consider French knitting, which takes less skill and practice.

> You will need: old-fashioned wooden cotton reels, each with four nails tapped into one end so that they protrude; wool; crochet hook or thick needle. You can also buy French knitting dollies quite cheaply from craft shops or on the internet.

Make it

Poke one end of the wool down through the hole in the cotton reel, with the ball of wool at the same end of the reel as the nails. Tie a loose knot round one of the nails and wrap the wool round the nails as shown in the diagram opposite. Then work the wool round each nail in turn (clockwise or anticlockwise), pulling the lower thread up and over the nail, towards the hole in the middle. Eventually a thick 'knitted' braid will appear through the hole in the cotton reel (you will need to help it along by pulling gently on the end of the braid).

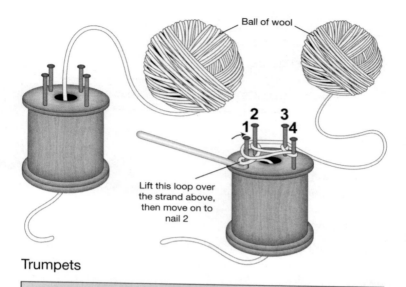

Ball of wool

2 3
1 4

Lift this loop over
the strand above,
then move on to
nail 2

Trumpets

You will need: card cut into quadrant shapes (a quadrant is a
quarter of a circle) for making trumpets; pens to decorate; sticky
tape and/or staples.

Make it

Show the children how the quadrant shapes of card can be rolled
to create trumpets. Invite them to decorate a card shape, then roll
up the trumpets ensuring that there is a hole at the top to toot
through.

Use the instruments to create an accompaniment to a song:
the children could take turns with singing and playing. You may
wish to supplement the card trumpets with ready-made percussion
instruments, or keep up the tooting theme by using kazoos.

Chat about it

How might trumpets have helped Gideon win the battle? What was
the most important advantage Gideon had?

Games

Water-drinking game

You will need: disposable plastic bowls; drinking water.

Play it

It is best to play this game before telling the story of Gideon's army. Put some water into the bowls and ask the children to try drinking without picking the bowls up. Watch to see how people do it.

Chat about it

Who would have gone home and who would have helped Gideon? Did it matter, or was the water-drinking test just a way to reduce the number of soldiers?

Wet wool experiment

You will need: real untreated sheep's wool; bowls of water; spray bottles; newspaper.

Do it

Show the children the raw wool and allow them to touch it. With the children, dip some wool in the water and see what happens. Next, place some dry wool on newspaper and try to spray the wool with water without wetting the paper.

Chat about it

Talk about the part that the wool plays in the story of Gideon. Was Gideon's need for proof understandable? Would we like God to prove himself to us, and would we believe it if he did?

Prayers

Noisy prayers

As Gideon's battle was a noisy affair, noisy prayers seem appropriate here. Encourage the children to be active: you could use their ideas or have suggestions of your own, for which the children could supply the actions. You could also use the trumpets that the children have made.

Here is an example.

We can stamp our feet (children stamp feet)
Thank you, God.
We can clap our hands (children clap hands)
Thank you, God.
We can snap our fingers (children snap fingers)
Thank you, God.
We can shout to you…
Thank you, God! Amen

You might want to finish with a quiet moment to pray for those who find it hard to maintain their faith or for those who doubt their worth or place in God's plan.

The story of Rahab

Key Bible focus

'I know that the Lord has given Israel this land. Everyone shakes with fear because of you... We know that the Lord your God rules heaven and earth, and we've lost our courage and our will to fight.'
JOSHUA 2:9, 11

The story of the woman who showed great bravery to protect her family by shielding Israelite spies has all the elements of a thriller. It forms part of the story of Joshua fighting the battle of Jericho.

The story of Rahab is found in Joshua 2 and 6. Many Bibles say that Rahab was a prostitute, but this may not necessarily have been the case. She could have been an ordinary woman or perhaps an innkeeper. The first part of the story, in chapter 2, tells how Rahab hid the Israelite spies in her house, making a deal with them to ensure her and her family's safety and helping them to escape. In the second part (chapter 6), the Israelites defeat Jericho and honour their side of the bargain.

Read the story of Rahab from a children's Bible or Bible storybook.

You might try hot-seating one of the children as Rahab to explore why she acted as she did. If the children are not familiar with hot-seating, you may need to take the chair to show them how to do it for the first few questions. (You can read a 'hot-seating' story in the chapter on Esther, later in this book.)

- Rahab showed great courage in helping the men to escape. She put herself in danger in order to save her family. Can you think of anyone else in the Bible who was just as brave in facing danger to save his friends and family from death?

Displays for the church

You might try the following large-scale weaving project or you could simply festoon a few lengths of red cord or ribbon around the church and attach the children's prayers to it. If you are using this session around the time of Remembrance, the themes of Rahab's story would chime well with more recent stories of heroism, in which people have risked their safety during war, for the lives of others.

Weaving with red cord

You will need: a frame of some sort (if you have a competent Scout or Guide to hand, they could make a rustic one by lashing sticks or short branches together to form a sturdy rectangle); red string or cord; strips of fabric or paper; screw-eyes (optional).

Make it

You will need to prepare the frame in advance by attaching the red cord to form vertical parallel lines. The distance between the lines will depend on the thickness of the string, the size of the frame and the size and weight of fabric or paper strips that you are using for the weaving. Remember that the children will need to be able to feed the strips in and out of the gaps between the string with their fingers. The threads can be attached by tying them around the frame or through holes in it, or you could use screw-eyes screwed into the sides.

Invite the children to weave the fabric or paper strips in and out of the strings, weaving over and under alternate strings on each pass across the frame to create a basket-weave effect. If you're feeling really artistic, you might discuss whether you want some kind of design and how to achieve it—perhaps graduating the colours from top to bottom.

Chat about it

While you work, you could discuss the story. Rahab hid the spies under the flax that was drying on her roof, so she may have been intending to spin and weave the flax. If you want to move outside the story, weaving is good metaphor for the way God weaves our lives together with other people's lives, just as he unexpectedly wove Rahab's life together with the lives of the Israelites.

City walls

> You will need: a large sheet of paper (lining paper or other plain wallpaper would do nicely); paint in different shades of brown, grey and red; sponges cut into rectangles (or ready-cut rectangular scouring pad sponges); shallow trays to hold the paint.

Make it

Unroll the paper on a surface (perhaps the floor, in which case you may need plastic sheeting to protect it) where the children can work. Show them how they can use the sponges and paint to print rectangular shapes, and how to arrange the shapes so that they look like a wall. Explain that they will need to leave gaps between the 'stones' or 'bricks' for the mortar joints. Invite the children to cover the paper in printed bricks or stones, varying the colours across the wall to give it an authentic look.

While the paint is drying, talk about the people who protect us (such as parents, nurses, street cleaners, policemen, and so on). When it is dry, write these suggestions on to the bricks. You might finish the display with a Bible verse.

Chat about it

Who protects us from harm? How do they protect us? Why do they do this? How did Rahab protect the people she loved? Whom should we protect and how? In what way does God protect us?

(This may be more to do with strengthening us to deal with trouble than insulating us from it.)

Craft activities

Friendship bracelets

> You will need: fine cord, wool or embroidery thread (some of it could be red).

Make it

This is just one way to make braids. You could use any other method you know and prefer.

You will be using three strands of thread. You could use multiple strands, but they must be arranged in three groups. Using three different colours will give a more interesting effect. Cut the threads to about 75cm.

X   Y   Z

Tie the threads together a little way down from one end and tape or tie the short ends to a solid object. Holding the middle strand (Y) with one hand, loop the left-hand thread (X) over the middle one, up and underneath it, and pull through towards the right (see the diagram). Pull tight and repeat, knotting the same strands in the same pattern. Strand X will now be in the middle.

Now loop the new middle strand (X) over and underneath the right hand strand (Z), up and underneath it and through towards the right. Pull tight and repeat with the same strands. Strand X will now be at the right and strand Y on the left. Start again from the left, looping strand Y over and under the middle strand (Z) twice, then over and under the right-hand strand (X) twice, pulling each knot tight as you go.

Continue in this way until you have made a braid of the required length to make a bracelet.

This activity is more suitable for older children. If you think it might take too long or require too great a degree of dexterity from the children, you could use single lengths of fine red cord and some attractive beads to string along the cord instead.

Chat about it

The Israelite spies found friends in unexpected places. Just as Rahab befriended them, they returned the favour. Helping each other is what friendship is about.

Hidden spies

You will need: sturdy card; mounting board cut to size (enough for two pieces for each child); materials for drawing and colouring; fine cord or thick thread; awl; darning needle; masking tape.

Make it

The mounting board should be cut with an aperture so that it will frame a photograph-sized picture. You will need two of these for each child. The sturdy card will need to be cut so that it is a little larger than the aperture in the mounting board.

Give each child a piece of card and invite them to draw a picture of the inside of Rahab's house on one side, and a picture of the two spies on the other, making sure that the bottom edge is the same for both pictures. When the pictures are finished, they can be slid between the two mounting boards and taped in place on one side so that they will not slip. Both sides of the card should now be framed by a mounting board.

Use the awl to make two holes in the top edge and another two in the bottom edge, through both mounting boards. Use the darning needle to pull a loop of thread through each pair of holes. Tie the ends of the loops so there is one loop at the top and another at the bottom of the picture.

Ask one child to hold the picture by its loops while another child turns it around its vertical axis a few times to twist the threads. When the picture is released and the two loops are gently pulled, the picture should flick round and round so quickly that the two spies appear to be inside the room.

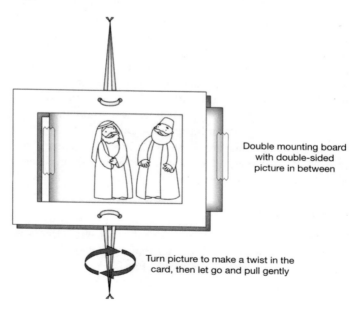

Double mounting board
with double-sided
picture in between

Turn picture to make a twist in the
card, then let go and pull gently

Chat about it

Talk about what it might have been like to be concealed in Rahab's house while the soldiers were searching it. How do you think the two Israelites felt while they were waiting?

Games

Secret writing

> You will need: paper and pens or pencils; *either* lemon juice, candle and matches *or* white candles, warm water and ink or watery paint.

Play it

Spies might have to send secret messages, so make your own secret writing. Ask the children either to devise codes with which to send secret messages, or to use lemon juice to write messages or draw pictures. The lemon juice will dry and become invisible, but it can be revealed when it is singed by a candle flame. Don't let the children do this themselves! If you do it, make sure you have a flameproof surface, with sand and water nearby. Practise beforehand so that you can judge how close to the flame you need to hold the paper without burning the children's work.

If using lemon juice and flame is too scary, you could write with wax candles softened in hot water, and wash ink or watery paint over the top to reveal the messages.

Hide and seek

This game needs no explanation. Link it to the way Rahab's visitors hid from the soldiers, both on her roof and, after their escape, in the hills. If you have the right sort of space in which to play, you could play a game of sardines or a more dynamic game, best played outside, where the children who are hiding have to make their way to a designated point without being seen or caught.

Prayers

String prayers

Try composing a string prayer, with the children taking turns to write the next line. This could be done without any particular plan, so that they write whatever they want to say, or you might try to obtain a more balanced prayer by planning with the children how the prayer will be structured. For instance, you might have four lines addressing God, followed by four lines confessing that we all do wrong sometimes, another four lines thanking God and a final four asking him for something.

If you want a visual representation, the lines can be written on strips of paper and fixed end-to-end. Could you write a long prayer to reach from the ceiling to the floor of your building?

Pegged prayers

Hang up a red ribbon or cord so that it dangles vertically. Talk to the children about times or circumstances when they might need courage—perhaps when it is difficult to do the right thing. Say that these are times when they might need some help (a rope) to scale a metaphorical wall.

Invite the children to write prayers about courage on pieces of paper. Use clothes pegs to attach the prayers to the red cord or ribbon.

The story of Samson

Key Bible focus

One day an angel from the Lord appeared to [Manoah's wife] and said: 'You have never been able to have any children, but very soon you will be pregnant and have a son. He will belong to God from the day he is born, so his hair must never be cut. And even before he is born, you must not drink any wine or beer or eat any food forbidden by God's laws. Your son will begin to set Israel free from the Philistines.'

JUDGES 13:3–5

The story of Samson has a lot to offer. Some people might be surprised at the behaviour of this Bible hero when reading the full story. However, the best-known part is full of drama, fighting and victory (of a sort) against the odds.

The story is found in Judges 13—16. The first part of it, at least, is crying out for enthusiastic audience participation, and a suggested script is printed below. Practise the responses to the words in bold before you begin: there are quite a few, but the children should soon get into the swing. It makes an excellent contrast to tell the first part of the story in this way, but leave Samson's final destruction of the Philistines' temple (and himself) to be told in a straightforward, sober way, perhaps at the end of the session.

- Samson used his strength to work for God. Sometimes we have to use not just physical strength but strength of mind as well. Can you think of someone in the Bible who didn't use his physical strength but used all his mental strength to work for God?

Samson and Delilah with audience participation

Responses

- **Samson**   'Hurray'
- **Philistines**   'Boo'
- **Delilah shouted** 'Samson, the Philistines are attacking'
- **Strong**   Biceps action
- **Secret**   Finger on lips
- **Weak**   Limp wrists
- **Hair**   Pat hair
- **Tie up/ties up**   Hold wrists together as though tied

Even though God rescued his people so often, they soon forgot about him. They worshipped the gods that other nations believed in, and before long they were in trouble again. Most often of all, trouble came from the **Philistines** in the south-west. For 40 years the **Philistines** ruled over the Israelites.

Then, one day, God sent a message to a man called Manoah and his wife, who lived in Zorah. 'You will have a son,' God said, 'who will grow up to deliver Israel from the **Philistines**.' When the boy was born, they called him **Samson** and they never cut his **hair**. It was a sign that **Samson** belonged to God in a special way. So **Samson** grew up and became very **strong**. You can read about all his victories over the **Philistines** in the Bible, in the book of Judges.

Samson fell in love with a Philistine woman named Delilah. The Philistine rulers went to Delilah and said, 'Trick **Samson** into telling you what makes him so **strong** and what can make him **weak**. Then we can **tie him up** so that he can't get away. If you find out his **secret**, we will each give you eleven hundred pieces of silver.'

The next time **Samson** was at Delilah's house, she asked,

'**Samson**, what makes you so **strong**? How can I **tie you up** so you can't get away? Come on, you can tell me your **secret**.' **Samson** answered, 'If someone **ties me up** with seven new bowstrings that have never been dried, it will make me just as **weak** as anyone else.'

The Philistine rulers gave seven new bowstrings to Delilah. They also told some of their soldiers to go to Delilah's house and hide in the room where **Samson** and Delilah were. If the bowstrings made **Samson weak**, they would be able to capture him.

Delilah **tied up Samson** with the bowstrings. **Delilah shouted**, 'Samson, the Philistines are attacking!' **Samson** snapped the bowstrings as though they were pieces of scorched string. The **Philistines** had not found out why **Samson** was so **strong**.

'You lied and made me look like a fool,' Delilah said. 'Now tell me your **secret**. How can I really **tie you up**?' **Samson** answered, 'Use some new ropes. If I'm **tied up** with ropes that have never been used, I'll be just as **weak** as anyone else.'

Delilah got new ropes and again some **Philistines** hid in the room. Then she **tied up Samson**'s arms. **Delilah shouted**, 'Samson, the Philistines are attacking!' **Samson** snapped the ropes as if they were threads.

'You're still lying and making a fool of me,' Delilah said. 'Tell me your **secret**. How can I **tie you up**?' **Samson** replied, 'If you weave my **hair** into the threads on a loom and nail the loom to a wall, then I will be as **weak** as anyone else.'

While **Samson** was asleep, Delilah wove his **hair** into the threads on a loom and nailed the loom to a wall. **Delilah shouted**, 'Samson, the Philistines are attacking!' **Samson** woke up and pulled the loom free, then he pulled his **hair** free from the woven cloth.

Delilah said, '**Samson**, you claim to love me, but you don't mean it! You've made me look like a fool three times now, and you still haven't told me your **secret**. Why are you so **strong**?' Delilah started nagging and pestering him day after day until he couldn't stand it any longer. Finally **Samson** told her the truth. 'I have belonged to God ever since I was born, so my **hair** has never been cut. If it were ever cut off, I would not be **strong** any longer; I would be as **weak** as anyone else.'

Delilah realised that he was telling the truth. So she sent someone to tell the Philistine rulers, 'Come to my house one more time. **Samson** has finally told me his **secret**.' The Philistine rulers went to Delilah's house, and they brought along the silver they had promised her.

Delilah had lulled **Samson** to sleep with his head resting in her lap. She began cutting off **Samson**'s **hair**. By the time she had finished, **Samson** was not **strong** any longer. Delilah **tied him up**. **Delilah shouted**, 'Samson, the Philistines are attacking!'

Samson woke up and thought, 'I'll break loose and escape, just as I always do.' He did not realise that the Lord had stopped helping him. The **Philistines** grabbed **Samson** and put out his eyes. They took him to the prison in Gaza and chained him up. Then they put him to work, turning a millstone to grind grain. But they didn't cut his **hair** any more, so it started growing back.

One day the Philistine rulers decided to throw a big party. Everyone was having a great time and they decided to bring out **Samson** as part of the entertainment, to make fun of him. They laughed and jeered at him. **Samson** told them he needed something to lean against, and, believing him to be just a blind, **weak** man, they allowed him to lean on the columns in the hall.

Samson prayed to God for strength one last time. He felt for two of the columns that were holding up the roof of the hall, and found one with each hand. Then he shouted, 'Let me die with the **Philistines**!' He pushed with all his might and the building collapsed with the **Philistines** and **Samson** still inside.

Displays for the church

Paper chains

You will need: plenty of strips of coloured paper; sticky tape; staples or glue to fasten the loops.

Make it

Show the children how to make paper loops, linking them together in a chain as you go. Invite them to make a good length of paper chain. You could use the chain for the prayer idea at the end of this chapter, then use it to decorate your room or the church.

Chat about it

Talk about what happened to Samson and why he was imprisoned. Discuss what it might be like to be chained up in prison. Try to draw out other ways that people can be trapped and unable to escape. Talk about how faith in God might be able to help people in those situations.

Craft activities

Flick books

You will need: small cheap notebooks (preferably unlined paper); pencils and/or pens.

Make it

Show the children how to create a flick book by drawing characters on one corner of the page, changing the character slightly on each page so that, as you flick through, they appear to move. If you start on the back page, when you turn the next page over it, the previous drawing will show through, enabling you to trace the drawing and easily make a small amendment for movement.

Encourage the children to make their own flick books showing part of Samson's story: the movement could be as simple as Samson's hair growing and then being cut off.

Grass-head people

> You will need: old (but clean) feet cut from tights; grass seed; sawdust; googly eyes; craft foam to decorate; waterproof glue; instructions for watering the grass head.

Make it

Mix the grass seed with a little sawdust. Show the children how to put a little of the mixture in the feet of the tights first, then stuff the rest of the sawdust on top to make a roughly round head shape. You will need to be careful to keep the seeded sawdust at the bottom, on the surface of the tights. Either tie off the tights with a knot or secure tightly with an elastic band. Glue on eyes, nose and other features as desired.

Show the children how, when they get home, they can stand their stocking head in a tray of water and wait for the hair to grow.

Chat about it

You might like to talk about why God connected Samson's strength with his hair. You might talk about how, sometimes, for religious reasons, people let their hair grow as a sign that they belong to God: they don't want to alter the way God created them.

Games

Demolition game

This game is more suitable for older children who will be mature enough not to be upset when their creation is destroyed.

> You will need: a plentiful supply of cardboard boxes and tubes (general junk modelling equipment, but some of the boxes will need to be on a larger scale than usual); two rolls of masking tape (or more if you have more than two teams).

Play it

Divide the children into two (or more) teams. Give each team a plentiful supply of cardboard boxes and tubes and a roll of masking tape. Their task is to make a structure (two pillars, floor and ceiling) large enough for someone to stand inside it: some of the cardboard boxes will need to be quite big. Give them a time limit, perhaps 20 minutes.

When the structures are finished, one member from the opposing team may stand inside the structure and see how quickly they can destroy it. Depending on the type of 'junk' you use, you might need to have some rules about the type of structure that can form the ceiling.

Arm wrestling competition

This needs no further explanation, but the children are likely to enjoy the contest!

Prayers

Chain prayers

Discuss with the children the sort of prayers that might be suitable for this story: perhaps they could pray especially for prisoners. Think about people who are imprisoned for their religious faith, or those who are unjustly imprisoned. Pray, too, for all prisoners, separated from their families and loved ones. Pray for those who are not literally in prison but feel imprisoned because of the sort of lives they lead: perhaps they are unable to escape poverty or are subject to oppression.

Using the paper chains made earlier in the session, wrap them round the group of children.

The children could take turns to say a prayer or you might have come up with a jointly written prayer from your discussion. You could conclude the prayers by asking God for strength to do his will: at the 'Amen', everyone could break free of the chain.

— Theme 6 —

The story of Ruth

Key Bible focus

Ruth answered, 'Please don't tell me to leave you and return home! I will go where you go, I will live where you live; your people will be my people, your God will be my God. I will die where you die and be buried beside you. May the Lord punish me if we are ever separated, even by death!'

RUTH 1:16–17

The book of Ruth tells a domestic story that is also about strong loyalty, perseverance in the face of adversity, and love.

The whole book is quite long, so you will almost certainly need to use a shorter version, picking out the key points for children. You could use a version from a children's Bible or, as the story has a quiet, intimate feel, it would work well retold in your own words, with the children sitting round in a circle.

- Because Ruth was Naomi's daughter-in-law, she chose to be part of God's family. We can choose to be part of God's family, too. Can you think of someone in the Bible who chose to be part of our human family so that we can all be God's children together?

Displays for the church

Make a larger version of the seed picture described in the craft activities below, perhaps creating a picture of a stalk (or a few stalks) of corn. You will need to use a board thick and strong enough to take the weight of the glue and seeds.

Although it is not strictly a 'display' for church, you could consider using a roll made in the bread-making activity at your next Communion service. In this way, your activities will become part of the wider life of the church.

Craft activities

Corn dollies

If you know how to make corn dollies, this would fit in well with the story of Ruth. If you can't obtain real corn, you could use art straws instead.

Plaster of Paris corn moulds

You will need: a good sized lump of Plasticine® or firm play dough for each child; ears of wheat or other grain (under-ripe ones are best as they won't fall apart so easily); cardboard strips cut to approximately 3–4cm wide (card from a cereal box is ideal); sticky tape; plaster of Paris; water; a container for mixing the plaster.

Make it

Show the children how to press the Plasticine® or play dough out flat, but not too thin (about 1.5–2cm thick should do), so that the top is smooth and reasonably level. Give the children a selection of ears of wheat or similar crop and show them how to make impressions of the ears of wheat by pressing them into the Plasticine®. Invite the children to do the same, making their own pattern of wheat. Encourage them to make 'clean' impressions by being careful when pressing into the Plasticine® and removing the wheat. Ensure that it is not pushed in too hard, so that there is plenty of modelling material left underneath the impressions and the wheat can be removed without leaving fingernail marks.

Each child will need to make a barrier using the card strips and sticky tape. The barrier will need to be big enough to encircle the design. Press the barrier firmly into the Plasticine®, around the design. Then mix up the plaster of Paris with water, according to the instructions on the packet, and pour the mixture into the card ring. When it is dry, the Plasticine® and card can be removed, leaving a positive image of the corn. This can be painted if desired, or left as plain plaster.

Chat about it

You might want to talk about the importance of cereals in our diet. What foods do we eat that contain wheat or other cereals? How important might it have been to people living in the time of Ruth?

Make sure the children understand that 'gleaning' means picking up the fallen grain that the harvesters had dropped or left behind. What might it have been like to depend on gleaning fallen corn from the fields to survive? How much grain might someone need to find, and how long might it take?

Bird scarers

You will need: pieces of plastic (plastic milk bottles, cut up, are ideal: the 4 or 6 pint ones are best and can be cut successfully with a modelling knife); acrylic paint; paintbrushes; plastic drinking straws; insulation tape; beads; Plasticine®; thin garden canes; ribbon or wool; large flashy sequins.

Make it

You will need to prepare three tailless cat shapes for each child (see the template in Appendix 3). The shapes should be cut from the plastic. Each cat needs to have triangular cuts down its side, which are opened out slightly. Paint the cats in bright colours, using acrylic paint: they will probably need two coats but, as the plastic is opaque, you will only need to paint one side.

To assemble the bird scarers, give each child three cat shapes. Invite them to stick on a sparkly sequin for each cat's eye and a piece of ribbon or plaited wool for the tail. They will need to tape a piece of plastic drinking straw to the back (the unpainted side) of each cat, using the insulation tape. Thread the cats on to a garden cane, using beads above and below each piece of drinking straw, held in place by blobs of Plasticine®, so that the cats are free to spin.

You may need to experiment in advance of your session to find the right diameter of bead. Alternatively, try cutting 'washers' from the leftover milk-bottle plastic so that the cats move freely. Remember to put a lump of Plasticine® or another sort of guard over the tip of the cane to protect eyes.

When the wind (or child) blows, the cats should swing round.

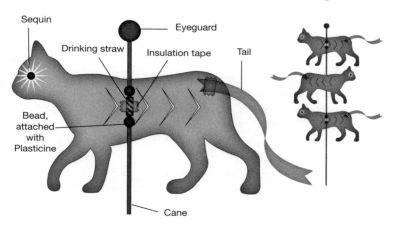

If the idea described above requires too much preparation, you could make a simple windmill. These can be bought in kit form or cut from card.

Use a square of card, cut diagonally towards the centre but leaving the central part of the square intact. Bend (but don't fold) alternate corners into the centre. Pass a pin through each corner and the central point of the windmill. Wiggle the pin a little to loosen up the windmill so that it will spin. Pin it into a wooden batten so that it spins freely when the wind blows. The windmills can be painted in bright colours.

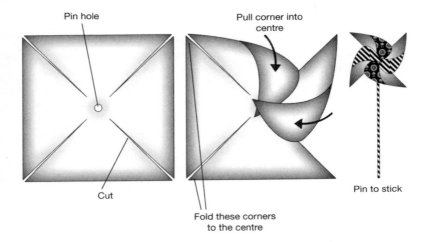

Pin hole

Pull corner into centre

Cut

Fold these corners to the centre

Pin to stick

Chat about it

Why would it be important to keep birds away from the crop, particularly for the people in Ruth's story who were gleaning grain in the fields?

Seed pictures

> You will need: a wide range of different seeds or dried pulses, such as lentils, split peas, sunflower seeds, pumpkin seeds and pearl barley (making sure different sizes and colours are represented); thick card; PVA glue; string.

Make it

Invite the children to sketch a design on to their card. Encourage them to keep it really simple, with large areas to fill, rather than lots of fiddly little areas. An ear of corn or a flower or snail might make good designs; abstract patterns are also very effective. It is a good idea to keep areas of the design separate by sticking string over the sketched lines.

Show the children how to spread a layer of glue over each separate area of the picture and then shake the seeds or pulses into the area. (Larger seeds may be individually placed.) With smaller seeds, the excess can be shaken off and collected for reuse in much the same way as glitter.

Chat about it

You might like to talk about the different types of food represented and what they all have in common. Perhaps you could talk about who grows them and where, and who eats them. Take care that the children don't eat raw dried pulses.

Cooking

Making bread

A bread recipe is provided in Appendix 2, but you could use any bread recipe you like.

> You will need: ingredients; bowls; baking parchment; baking trays; hot oven; hand-washing facilities (washing-up bowl with warm water, soap and towels).

Ensure that the children have clean hands before they begin. Invite them to make the bread together. With kneading and rising time, this will take a while, so, if you have insufficient time, you could have a quantity of bread dough ready for the children to shape into rolls or plaits. If you have access to cooking facilities, the finished bread could be shared later in the session. Alternatively, children could take their dough home with instructions on how to bake it.

Games

Hunt the wheat ear

Ruth spent a lot of time gleaning corn—looking for loose ears of corn in the field, which the reapers had missed. To remember this, you could play a version of hunt the thimble—perhaps with more than one 'thimble'.

> You will need: small pictures of ears of wheat (you might use pictures printed from clip art if you have a computer, laminated to ensure that you can use them again).

Play it

Hide the pictures in the room or space you use, or, for greater realism, on a fine day you could scatter them outside. Keep a note of how many you have hidden.

Invite the children to find as many pictures as they can. For safety, you may need to talk to them about places where they will not need to (and should not) hunt for the wheat.

Chat about it

Relate the experience to looking for tiny grains of wheat fallen to the ground in the fields. What sort of an experience might that have been?

Prayers

Mapped-out prayers

Spend some time discussing where our food comes from and identify the places on a map so that you can pray for each place.

Grain offerings

You could use the pictures of wheat ears used in the 'Hunt the wheat ear' game to place in a bowl or on the altar, or in the centre of the group, as each prayer is offered. Of course, real ears of wheat could also be used.

As each ear of wheat is placed, pray for all people who produce our food and get it into our shops. Pray for all the farm workers and farm owners who work so hard in all weathers so that we can be fed. Pray also for places where farming is much harder, where failure of the crop is a regular occurrence and where farmers have lost their livelihoods. Pray for the organisations that help these people to start farming again and help them with the problems (such as lack of water) that they encounter.

— Theme 7 —

The story of David

Key Bible focus

Jesse sent all seven of his sons over to Samuel. Finally, Samuel said, 'Jesse, the Lord hasn't chosen any of these young men. Do you have any more sons?' 'Yes,' Jesse answered. 'My youngest son David is out taking care of the sheep.' 'Send for him!' Samuel said. 'We won't start the ceremony until he gets here.' Jesse sent for David. He was a healthy, good-looking boy with a sparkle in his eyes. As soon as David came, the Lord told Samuel, 'He's the one! Get up and pour the olive oil on his head.' Samuel poured the oil on David's head while his brothers watched. At that moment, the Spirit of the Lord took control of David and stayed with him from then on.

1 SAMUEL 16:10–13

There are many stories about David in the Bible, depicting him in a number of different lights. He knew a humble life looking after sheep but also an exalted one as king. He was a very human figure, as prone to temptation as anyone else but with many laudable qualities and capable of great friendship and faith. King David is one of the most important figures in Jewish history—famous as a great king, a poet, a musician and a warrior.

Read a story from the life of David from a children's Bible or Bible storybook. You will need to select the best story for your purposes. The version of the story of David and Goliath with audience participation given on pages 70–71 highlights David's reliance on God. The story of how David was chosen as king is found in 1 Samuel 16, immediately before the story about Goliath. It shows how God often surprises us with his choice of people to take part in his plan. You might also consider telling the story of David's great friendship with Jonathan (1 Samuel 18—31).

The Psalms

A session on David would be incomplete without telling the children about David the psalm writer. It is worth showing them where the book of Psalms is in the Old Testament, and explaining that psalms are a mixture of prayer, poem and song addressing God. They are true to the psalmist's feelings at the time they were written, so they can be joyful and thankful or angry and despairing, but they are always honest with God about whatever emotion they express.

Psalms are still either said or sung in some church services as part of worship today, thousands of years after the biblical psalms were written. Read a few to the children. You could consider a selection from the following:

- ❖ Psalm 22:1–8 (calling for God)
- ❖ Psalm 23 (this one might be familiar to them)
- ❖ Psalm 74:1–2, 10–11 (expressing despair and the hope that enemies will be punished)
- ❖ Psalm 123 (requesting mercy)
- ❖ Psalm 131 (expressing trust in God)
- ❖ Psalm 136:1–9 (expressing confidence in God)
- ❖ Psalm 139:1–18 (describing how well God knows us)
- ❖ Psalm 143:1–6 (asking for help in times of despair)
- ❖ Psalm 150 (a song of praise)

- The stories about David and the Psalms that he wrote show that God was always with David, even when David had done something wrong, or when he was unhappy or frightened. Can you think of someone else in the Bible who knew God was always with him?
- Can you think of someone who has promised that God is always with us?

David and Goliath with audience participation

The story of David and Goliath may be unfamiliar to more children than you might imagine. It has the obvious attraction of the triumph of the underdog, winning against all odds. Children especially enjoy the idea of a boy getting the better of an adult. Try telling it using audience participation, as below. Ask the children to practise doing the actions or making the noises at the appropriate moments in the story (shown in bold text).

- **David**   'Hurray'
- **Goliath**   'Boo'
- **Sheep**   'Baaa'
- **Sling**   Wave arm round above head
- **Stone(s)**   'Ouch'
- **Fight**   Cross forearms
- **Strong**   Flex biceps

Although **David** was only a young boy, he looked after his father's **sheep** out on the hills. **David** was brave and fought off the wild animals that tried to steal the **sheep**, even the fierce lions and bears. He led the **sheep** over the hills to find the best grass for them. While **David** watched them, he practised firing **stones** with his **sling** and playing his harp.

One day **David**'s father sent him to take food to his brothers, who were soldiers in King Saul's army. For years, Saul had been **fight**ing the Philistines. Now their armies were camped on either side of the valley, watching each other and not daring to attack.

One Philistine soldier was a giant of a man called **Goliath**. He was tremendously **strong** and wore a great helmet and breastplate. He carried a huge shield and a heavy spear. Every day he shouted across the valley to King Saul's army, 'Send one of your **strong**est men to **fight** with me. Whoever wins the **fight** wins the battle for his whole army.'

King Saul's army listened to **Goliath**'s challenge but all the men were too scared to go. When **David** reached the army camp, he heard **Goliath** shouting. He said to King Saul, 'I'll go and **fight**.' 'You're only a boy. **Goliath** is a trained soldier,' said King Saul. 'I'm not afraid,' said **David**. 'When I was looking after my father's **sheep**, I killed bears and lions with God's help. God will look after me now because **Goliath** wants to kill God's people.'

'You may go,' said King Saul, 'but you must wear my **fight**ing clothes and take my sword.' **David** put them on but they were much too big and heavy for him, so he took them off again. **David** picked up his shepherd's stick and chose five small **stones** from a stream for his **sling**. Then he strode down the valley to **fight Goliath**.

When **Goliath** saw **David** coming, he made fun of him and shouted, 'Come here, boy, and I will kill you.'

David walked on. 'You have a sword and a spear but I have God to help me,' he said. Then **David** put one of the little **stones** in his **sling**, swung the **sling** round his head and let it go.

The **stone** shot out of the **sling**, straight at **Goliath**. The **stone** hit the giant right in the middle of his forehead. **Goliath** fell down on the ground. The **stone** had killed him. **David** ran up to **Goliath** and saw that he was dead.

When the Philistine army saw their **strong**est warrior lying on the ground, they all ran away. King Saul's army celebrated the victory that, with God's help, **David** had won for them.

Performance for the church

Setting and performing a psalm

Choose a psalm and read it to the children. It could be one of the psalms suggested above or one of your choosing. Then ask them to create some music to go with the psalm. You may have some gifted musicians in your group, but don't worry if you haven't. If you choose a psalm carefully, simple percussion instruments will be effective.

Decide which sounds will be needed where, and when the voice reading the psalm needs to pause. You could also use different voices for different parts of the psalm—for instance, a single voice for some lines, and a group for others. The music is to give the psalm texture: the words shouldn't be drowned out. The finished psalm setting could be performed to the wider congregation.

If you prefer, invite the children to write their own modern-day psalm. Look at a few contrasting examples in the Bible first. Discuss how psalms are worship songs to God but stress that there is a lot of variety in the types of things people want to say to God. Some psalms are amazingly joyful, while others are despairing.

Make notes of some ideas for your own psalm (or children could work individually if they prefer) and write a psalm as a group, using the children's ideas. Perhaps they will want to thank God for his gifts and bounty, or perhaps they will want to ask him why he allows poverty. The key is to be honest.

Craft activities

Glass harmonica

You will need: water; glass containers (bottles or drinking glasses).

Make it

There are two ways to approach this activity. Using glass bottles filled with different amounts of water, you could tap them gently to produce different notes (or blow over the tops gently to get a more flutey sound). Alternatively, with older and well-coordinated children, you could use glasses filled with different amounts of water. A wet finger rubbed round and round the rim of the glass will produce a singing note.

As glass is being used here, of course, caution will be required and you will need a plan in place for how to handle breakages. Do test drinking glasses to check that they 'sing' well, as some are easier to get a note out of than others.

Chat about it

Discuss the kind of sounds your instruments produce. Could we use this sound to accompany a psalm? How many different notes can we produce?

Marbling

> You will need: a water tray; water; marbling ink (available from craft shops); paper; a plastic spoon.

Make it

As the marbling technique involves floating oil on water, this activity fits well with the story of David being anointed by Samuel when he was identified as the future king.

Follow any instructions with the marbling equipment you have, but the basic technique is to pour water into the tray, 2–3cm deep. Ask the children to write their name on their piece of paper. In turns, they will each need to choose which colour inks they want to use. It is best to use no more than three colours for each piece of paper. Add a dose of each of the chosen coloured inks and give a very gentle swirl with a spoon if required. Then invite the children to lay their paper very gently on top of the water. It's a good idea to take a second 'copy' to use up any remaining ink before the next child has a go. Remove the paper after a couple of seconds, allow the water to drip back into the tray and hang the paper to dry.

You will need to experiment before the session starts so that you can judge how much ink you need for each paper.

Chat about it

Why do you think kings were anointed with oil? Why would it show that they were special in some way?

Oil pastel pictures

You will need: oil pastels; good-quality paper.

Invite the children to illustrate David's story using the oil pastels or even to draw images associated with kingship. Show the children that they can experiment with blending colours on the paper and smudging to obtain interesting effects. Oil pastels can be quite messy, so you are likely to need hand-washing equipment too.

Games

Chocolate eating game

You will need: large bars of chocolate (one for each team); a set of unwieldly clothing for each team (including a pair of large gloves, a hat big enough to fall over a child's face, and a bulky overcoat); a knife and fork for each team.

Play it

Divide the children into teams and give each team a knife and fork and a set of clothes. Each team member in turn puts on all the clothing and then sits down to eat the bar of chocolate with the knife and fork. If you prefer, you could provide a knife and fork for each child.

You will need some rules for the game. Chocolate is only to be eaten one square at a time, and it must on no account be touched by anything other than the knife and fork. The team member who is doing the eating must be fully clothed at all times. Each team member has only an agreed amount of time for his or her go—perhaps one or two minutes, which will include the time needed for changing clothes. The time may need to be varied depending on the age of the children.

Chat about it

The game is great fun, and afterwards you could relate the children's experience to David's reasons for rejecting the heavy suit of armour he was offered before he fought Goliath.

Discussion activities

Choosing a king

You could use this discussion activity as an introduction to the story of how David was chosen as king. Talk with the children about how we might recognise a king. What might a king look like? What might he wear? How can you tell if someone is important? Come up with a list of things: a king might wear a crown, be at the centre of a crowd, wear expensive clothing, have guards to protect him, sit on his throne in a palace, have people to cook his food, mend his clothes and run his bath, and so on.

You might then compare your list with the story about David. Would anyone have been able to tell that David would be a king? Why might God have chosen him? It is encouraging to know that God can and does work with extremely unpromising material.

Prayers

Candle prayers

Candles can be a symbol of God with us, and Jesus as the light of the world. You might like to use this symbolism to pray for people who are facing 'impossible' odds in their work, as David did. You could include people who are working to end poverty or combat disease, or those working for peace between peoples who have been enemies for a very long time, or people who are persecuted as David was persecuted by King Saul. The children will probably have their own suggestions, or may personally know someone who qualifies.

Children could take turns to light a candle, or a candle could be lit as they take turns to say their prayer.

Musical prayers

Taking inspiration from the psalms, you could use a bell or chime bar during prayers. After each prayer, strike a single note and allow the sound to die away before saying the next prayer.

If you're musical, you could teach the children a simple Taizé chant to sing in between each prayer sentence.

Meditation on Psalm 23

Try this guided visualisation with the children. It may take some practice to accustom them to sitting still and listening without fidgeting, but it is worth it if you can persevere. Read the meditation slowly and quietly, allowing pauses for the children to imagine and reflect.

Try to sit comfortably—back straight, shoulders relaxed, feet on the floor. Close your eyes and remember the colour of the sky on a bright, clear, sunlit day. Think of the sun travelling across the sky, turning the sky through all the different shades of blue.

It starts with deepest blue, studded with stars and perhaps a round, pale, glowing moon. As the sky begins to lighten, the grey of twilight creeps over the horizon, making everything seem black and white, but, as the sun begins to rise and a few wispy clouds gather, the sky turns to a glowing polished bronze, deepening as the sun appears to a flaming orange, fading into pink and turquoise. The sky looks newly washed and polished as gradually the sun turns from boiling orange to pale white. The sky loses its pink tinge and turns a beautiful translucent powder blue, brighter at the zenith and glowing a deeper blue towards the horizon.

Imagine yourself, on such a day, setting out for a walk. You feel the comfortable warmth of the sun on your back and a gentle breeze playing around your face. It is spring, and you walk towards the countryside.

As you walk, you meet the person you know and trust the best in all the world. Imagine them clearly. This person will be your guide. Your guide takes you by the hand. Feel the warmth and reassurance of that hand holding yours, and walk willingly with your guide.

You walk along a riverbank. The grass is springy, green and fragrant. It has the freshness of the morning but is not damp. The river is clean and glitters. It follows its path lazily and calmly. Think about the creatures that depend on this meadow and the river—the insects, birds and mammals that live here. What sounds do you hear as you walk along? What scents do you sniff along the riverbank? Enjoy your walk with your guide.

As you continue your walk, you notice the sky beginning to darken. The banks of the river steepen and the water takes on the dull grey colour of the clouds overhead. The path continues by the river but cliffs begin to rise on the other side. The soft grass gives way to jagged stones, which are difficult to walk over and shift and slip uneasily as you put weight on them.

As the sky becomes heavy with clouds and prickles with the threat of a storm, the cliffs rise beside you. You feel shut in and oppressed. You grip your guide's hand more tightly and are answered with the warm, comforting pressure of their hand. As you feel more and more threatened, you lean on your guide's arm and find it strong, reassuring and dependable. You look at your guide's face and realise that nothing can harm you while you are in their presence; you gain strength and renewal from this realisation.

Eventually the path evens out, your feet find firmer ground, and the walking becomes easier. The sky brightens with evening light. You see the most marvellous building in the distance. Imagine what it looks like. What size is it? What is it made from? What colour is it?

As you get closer, you realise that your guide is leading you to this place. Think about how the details of doors, windows and gardens become clearer and clearer. There is a warm and welcoming light at the windows and you reach the door as the first few stars appear in the sky above you. Your guide leads you inside and welcomes you. There is a bright fire to warm yourself by and a table prepared for a meal. Your favourite food and drink is on that table. Imagine what it looks like and smells like.

Your guide invites you to sit and eat. You find that there are friends here. Take a while to enjoy the feast. You know that you are welcome to stay as long as you wish. Even if you leave that place for a while, in some way you will be able to take the feeling that you have there with you.

Now we need to return to our room, so get up from the feast and look out of the window. Watch as the night sky slowly turns to grey twilight and the sun begins to rise once more. See how the sky begins to look like polished metal as it turns a pearly gold, then pink, and finally a translucent powder blue.

When you are ready, you can open your eyes and have a stretch.

— Theme 8 —

The story of Solomon

Key Bible focus

One night while Solomon was in Gibeon, the Lord God appeared to him in a dream and said, 'Solomon, ask for anything you want, and I will give it to you.' Solomon answered: 'My father David, your servant, was honest and did what you commanded. You were always loyal to him, and you gave him a son who is now king. Lord God, I'm your servant, and you've made me king in my father's place. But I'm very young and know so little about being a leader. And now I must rule your chosen people, even though there are too many of them to count. Please make me wise and teach me the difference between right and wrong. Then I will know how to rule your people. If you don't, there is no way I could rule this great nation of yours.'

1 KINGS 3:5–9

In many ways the figure of Solomon is quite a contrast with his father, King David. This is no rags-to-riches story. Instead, Solomon seems to glitter from the beginning: not only does he have great wealth and power but God also endows him with legendary wisdom, as many of his proverbs bear witness (although, according to 2 Kings 11, this wisdom may have failed him when he got older). In addition to his capacity for wisdom, he is best known as the builder of the temple in Jerusalem.

The stories about Solomon are found in both 1 Kings and 2 Chronicles. The story of God giving him wisdom could introduce a discussion with children about the nature of gifts, and what might be the best gift. Given the backdrop of wealth and splendour to the stories about Solomon, it is good to consider that the best gifts are even more precious and beyond price. This story is found in 1 Kings 3 and 2 Chronicles 1.

In the 1 Kings 3 version, the story goes on to tell about the wisdom of Solomon in operation, as he decides which of two women is the real mother of a baby. You could demonstrate Solomon's importance as a king by using the descriptions of the building of the temple in 1 Kings 5—6 and 2 Chronicles 2—5, which tell how lavish it was.

Proverbs

A session on Solomon provides the ideal opportunity to begin to explore the book of Proverbs, since (by tradition) many of the proverbs in it were written by Solomon. Show the children where to find the book in the Bible and select a few to read. Perhaps the children could think of some proverbs of their own, or you could use the games ideas described later in this chapter.

- Solomon asked God for the gift of wisdom so that he could rule wisely, but God's wisdom doesn't always seem wise to us. Can you think of someone who used God's wisdom but rejected human wisdom, to show us that the wisdom of God can seem to be foolishness?

Displays for the church

Solomon's temple

You will need: a large pre-prepared cardboard box; glue; paint; materials for modelling (such as card, clay, pipe cleaners and foil); materials for collage (plenty of shiny, bright cards and papers, and fabrics); pictures of what some of the items in the temple may have looked like (optional); card and a pen to make labels.

Make it

You will need to prepare the box in advance. Cut away one or two sides so that the inside is easy to see and access. You may need to glue some of the cardboard flaps back to ensure that the box is stable. It is a good idea to paint the box in white emulsion to give a good base for the children's collage.

Look carefully at the biblical descriptions of Solomon's temple and use them, together with plenty of imagination, to construct what the children think the temple might have looked like. Focus on the valuable materials used and the care that must have gone into making this spectacular building as special as possible for God. When it comes to the internal furnishings, such as the altar, bowl and lampstands, individual children or small groups might make the items ready to put inside the model.

When the temple is finished, write some labels using verses from the Bible (including references) and pin or stick them to the appropriate part of the model.

Craft activities

Pasta jewellery

You will need: straight pasta tubes; acrylic paint; glitter glue; paintbrushes; wool or thick thread; darning needle; scissors.

Make it

Paint the pasta tubes in bright colours and allow to dry. If you use acrylic paint and don't apply it too thickly, drying should not take very long. When the tubes are dry, they can be decorated with spots, zigzags or stripes, using either more paint or glitter glue. They can then be threaded on to the wool or thread to make necklaces. Beads could be added alongside the pasta tubes if desired.

Chat about it

Solomon had lots of fine treasures, in the temple and in his palace in Jerusalem. You might wonder what they looked like, and what Solomon might have done with them.

Solomon's coins

> You will need: circles cut from thick card, about 4–5cm diameter; pieces of thick tinfoil cut slightly larger than the card circles; strong glue (such as a glue gun); blunt pencils or ballpoint pens.

Make it

Show the children how to smooth the tinfoil around the card circles and then use a ballpoint pen or blunt pencil to engrave a design on the foil. Invite the children to create their own coin designs. They will need to create two designs for each coin. Use the glue to stick the two coin sides together.

Chat about it

Talk to the children about Solomon's riches. What would be a wise thing to do with all that money?

Treasure boxes

> You will need: a box with a lid for each child (small shoebox size, or plain card boxes available from craft shops); paint; paintbrushes; collage supplies (fake jewels, buttons, sequins, foil, gold paper and ribbon); glue; felt or other fabric to line the box.

Make it

Solomon must have had special boxes in which to keep his jewels and gold. What might they have looked like? Invite the children to decorate their boxes in whatever way seems best, so that they could keep something special inside. Remind them that the lid will need to fit on the box when they have finished, so they should avoid decorating the rim. The boxes can be lined with pieces of fabric to make them extra-special.

Chat about it

The finished boxes could be used as containers for the pasta jewellery or the coins—but remind the children of the more precious gift of wisdom, which Solomon asked God to give him. Invite them to write a prayer asking God for help with a particular gift, perhaps asking him for wisdom or kindness or joy. The children could keep this prayer in their box as a reminder that the best gifts cannot be purchased but are for God to give.

Wise old owls

> You will need: card marked (and cut if you prefer) into body shapes and wing shapes (use the template in Appendix 3); string; paint; paper fasteners; beads or buttons; hole punch; scissors; glue; paper/card/fabric scraps for eyes, beak and feet; darning needle.

Make it

The owls are not difficult to make, but it would be worth trying one out at home first to make it easier to judge where the wings hinge best.

Younger children might enjoy using their fingers to produce the speckled feather pattern on the owl's breast, and handprints to make the wings. Older children may prefer making and using (or just using ready-made) print blocks. Print blocks for the breast feathers could be made using the bubbly side of some bubble wrap.

For the wings, invite the children to write (following the direction in which the feathers would lie) names of the character gifts that

God gives, such as wisdom, compassion, kindness, understanding, grace, courage, and so on. Alternatively, the children could print from real feathers (robust tail feathers, rather than down) or corrugated card cut in feather shapes.

Invite the children to print a speckled pattern on the owl body using either print blocks or fingers. Then print the wings or write words for different gifts on them.

When the paint is dry, punch a hole at the top of the owl's head and thread a hanging loop through it. Punch another hole at the top of each wing. Use the darning needle to make two holes in the body where you want the wings to hinge, and another hole about one-third of the way down each wing. Fix each wing behind the body using paper fasteners, then loop some string through the punched holes on each wing (not too tightly) and knot it, leaving a length of string dangling down below the owl body. Knot a bead or button on the end of the string to weigh it down a little.

Complete the owl by adding eyes, a beak and feet cut from the scraps. When the owl is hung up and the string pulled gently, the wings should flap.

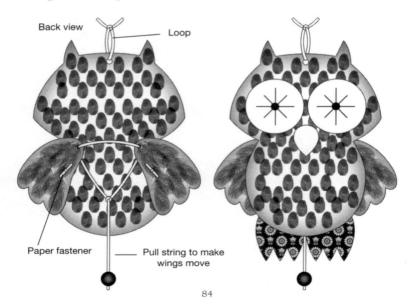

Back view

Loop

Paper fastener

Pull string to make wings move

Chat about it

We think of owls as symbols of wisdom, so, while the children are making them, you might like to talk about what wisdom is. How can you tell if someone is wise? Do you have to be clever to be wise? Do you know someone who is wise?

Games

Proverbs memory game (for older children)

> You will need: a selection of proverbs printed on A5 card; a small prize (optional).

Play it

Print each proverb on to a piece of card. (You might want to help the children to remember them by using different colours and/ or adding a picture to the words.) Tell the children that you will be reading the proverbs out during the session, and there will be a prize for the person who remembers the most. Read a different proverb—perhaps every 20 minutes, perhaps at a different location in your room—and leave the card there so that children can look at it.

At the end of the session, collect the cards (to prevent cheating) and invite the children to write down as many proverbs as they can remember. Give a prize for the longest list.

If you want to play this game with younger children or as a less competitive activity, don't offer a prize, but see how many proverbs the group as a whole can remember.

Matching proverbs

You will need: two colours of paper or card and a selection of verses from Proverbs (Proverbs 10 is a good place to start your search). Each proverb is split in half, with one half printed on one colour of paper and the other on the second colour: for example, if you were to choose Proverbs 10:17, you would print 'Accept correction, and you will find life' on, say, a blue slip of paper, and 'reject correction and you will miss the road' on a pink slip.

Play it

Arrange the slips of paper on a table and invite the children to decide which halves of the verses belong together. Remind them that they need to pair one of each colour. Choose some obvious pairs, along with some less obvious. Use a Bible to check whether the correct pairs have been chosen.

Solomon's shopping list

Use the shopping list game to build a list of what Solomon might have had in his temple. Children take turns to complete the sentence 'When Solomon built the temple, he used…'. Each time, another item is added to the list but all the preceding ideas have to be repeated. For example: 'When Solomon built the temple, he used the labour of thousands of men'; 'When Solomon built the temple, he used the labour of thousands of men and tons of glittering gold'; 'When Solomon built the temple, he used the labour of thousands of men, tons of glittering gold and shiny sea-blue turquoises', and so on.

Discussion activities

Best gift

Talk to the children about what they most want. If someone has a birthday coming up, or if Christmas is getting close, use these occasions to explore what might be most desirable. Solomon was given the option of choosing whichever gift he most wanted. Discuss what wisdom really is: can the children define it? Discuss Solomon's choice and why he might have made it.

If you could ask God for one special gift, what might it be?

Prayers

Precious prayers

Use highly polished stones or 'jewels' (mirror-backed plastic ones, which are also useful for collages) or clear glass pebbles. Place the polished stones or 'jewels' in a bowl and invite the children to choose one or a few of them. You might need to explain how they will be used so that the children don't think they will be keeping them.

You could say the prayers while the children hold their jewels— which, at the end, they place on a special plate or on the altar to symbolise offering their prayer. For older children, you could invite each child to say a line of the prayer while a plate is passed round the circle. As they say each line, they place one of the jewels on the plate.

If it is easier or you prefer it, you could try handing the jewels out as part of the prayers, as a thanksgiving for the wonderful gifts that God gives each of us. The children could then keep their jewels as a reminder of what God has given us.

Incense prayers

Incense would have been used in Solomon's temple, so why not try lighting an incense stick. Talk to the children about how people often thought of their prayers rising up to heaven with the smoke. Take a few moments to look at it and get used to the scent. Then say prayers.

Guided visualisation on gifts

Speak in a calm, slow voice, leaving plenty of pauses to give the children time to imagine the scene and their responses. Check that everyone is sitting comfortably, with backs straight but relaxed and eyes closed.

Start by listening hard. Listen to the furthest sound you can hear. It could be a plane in the sky or wind moving the trees, or the road outside. Then listen to closer sounds—the sounds you can hear in our room. Perhaps you can hear the clock ticking or the hum of the electric lights. Now listen to the sounds you can hear inside yourself—air entering and leaving your body, the sound of blood pumping in your ears.

Now I want you to imagine a present. You notice it—one small present sitting on the table. It looks as though it has been left there for you to find.

The present doesn't look very interesting. It's wrapped in smooth, plain brown paper and tied with string. You pick it up. The label says it is for you. Feel the texture of the wrapping in your hand. The tiny parcel is very light. You give it a small shake but hear nothing. You don't recognise the writing on the label.

You sit down with the gift and take your time to open it. You slowly pull the string to undo it, then carefully fold back the plain brown paper. Inside is a small box that fits easily into your hand. It is too small to hold any of the things you might have asked anyone to give you. Look at the box. Slowly you lift up the lid and look inside.

The box seems empty. Think about how this non-present makes you feel. Perhaps it means someone is playing a joke on you; perhaps it makes you feel disappointed or upset.

But look again. When you do, you realise that although it seems empty, nevertheless it contains the most wonderful gift. It is something you did not know you wanted or needed, something you never thought to ask for. Perhaps it's love, or peace, or friendship, or a helping hand, or something to rely on, or grace. Look at the gift. What might it look like, now that you can see it? What shape and size is it?

You realise that it is emitting the most beautiful soft, gentle light that seems to fill the room. Enjoy the effect of this light in the room. What colour is it? There's a soft but beautiful sound, too. You need to listen carefully to hear it, but, once you know it's there, it fills your head and heart. Enjoy the light and sound. You feel you could sit here for ever, just enjoying the feeling of that most perfect gift. Take a few minutes to enjoy the gift.

Now we need to come back to our room here, so listen to the sounds within your body—your gentle breathing, your pulse tapping. Listen to the sounds in the room with us—the clock ticking, the light humming. Now listen to the furthest sounds you can hear and, when you are ready, you can open your eyes and have a stretch.

— Theme 9 —

The story of Elijah

Key Bible focus

Elijah stretched himself out over the boy three times, while praying, 'Lord God, bring this boy back to life!' The Lord answered Elijah's prayer, and the boy started breathing again. Elijah picked him up and carried him downstairs. He gave the boy to his mother and said, 'Look, your son is alive.' 'You are God's prophet!' the woman replied. 'Now I know that you really do speak for the Lord.'
1 KINGS 17:21–24

The story of Elijah is all about integrity, faith, apparently insurmountable odds and natural disasters.

Read a story about Elijah from a children's Bible or Bible story book. The obvious stories to consider are Elijah being fed by the ravens and reviving the widow's son (1 Kings 17:1–24), the prophets of Baal (1 Kings 18:17–40), and God passing by in silence (1 Kings 19:9–18). You could use a story with actions or a guided visualisation: both kinds of story are given below.

• Elijah listened to God and realised that it can be hard to hear him speaking: Elijah heard him best in silence. Can you think of someone else in the Bible who went to quiet places, like the desert or the top of a hill, to be with God and listen?

Fed by ravens

Try this as a story with actions. The children will not be making any noise, just doing the following movements in response to certain words (shown in bold below).

- **Ravens:** flap arms
- **Brook:** move hands like rippling water
- **Rain:** move fingers down like raindrops
- **Lord:** hands praying
- **Flour:** hold out right hand, palm up
- **Oil:** hold out left hand, palm up
- **Son or boy:** hold out hand, palm down, as though touching a child's head

Elijah was a prophet from Tishbe in Gilead. One day he went to King Ahab and said, 'I'm a servant of the living **Lord**, the God of Israel, and I swear in his name that it won't **rain** until I say so. There won't even be any dew on the ground.'

Later the **Lord** said to Elijah, 'Leave and go across the River Jordan so that you can hide near Cherith **Brook**. You can drink water from the **brook** and eat the food I've told the **ravens** to bring you.'

Elijah obeyed the **Lord** and went to live near Cherith **Brook**. **Ravens** brought him bread and meat twice a day and he drank water from the **brook**. But after a while, it dried up because there was no **rain**.

The **Lord** told Elijah, 'Go to the town of Zarephath in Sidon and live there. I've told a widow in that town to give you food.'

When Elijah came near the town gate of Zarephath, he saw a widow gathering sticks for a fire. 'Would you please bring me a cup of water?' he asked. As she left to fetch it, he asked, 'Would you also please bring me a piece of bread?' The widow answered, 'In the name of the living **Lord** your God, I swear that I don't have any bread. All I have is a handful of **flour** and a little **olive oil**. I'm on my way home now with these few sticks to cook what I have for my **son** and me. After that, we will starve to death.'

Elijah said, 'Everything will be fine. Do what you said. Go home and prepare something for yourself and your **son**. But first, please make a small piece of bread and bring it to me. The **Lord** God of Israel has promised that your jar of **flour** won't run out and your bottle of **oil** won't dry up before he sends **rain** for the crops.'

The widow went home and did exactly as Elijah had told her. She and Elijah and her **son** had enough food for a long time. The **Lord** kept the promise that his prophet Elijah had made and she did not run out of **flour** or **oil**.

Several days later, the woman's **son** fell ill, and he kept getting worse until finally he died. The woman shouted at Elijah, 'What have I done to you? I thought you were the **Lord**'s prophet. Did you come here to cause the death of my **son** as a reminder that I've sinned against the **Lord**?'

'Bring me your **son**,' Elijah said. Then he took the **boy** from her arms and carried him upstairs to the room where he was staying. Elijah laid the **boy** on his bed and prayed, '**Lord** God, why did you do such a terrible thing to this woman? She's letting me stay here, and now you've let her **son** die.' Elijah stretched himself out over the **boy** three times while praying, '**Lord** God, bring this **boy** back to life!'

The **Lord** answered Elijah's prayer and the **boy** started breathing again. Elijah picked him up and carried him downstairs. He gave the **boy** to his mother and said, 'Look, your **son** is alive.'

'You are the **Lord**'s prophet!' the woman replied. 'Now I know that you really do speak for the **Lord**.'

Displays for the church

Performance stories

The children could prepare the dramatic narrative story of the prophets of Baal (1 Kings 18:17–40) to present to the wider congregation or for a concluding act of worship. This works well if the children are divided into two groups, one to take the part of Elijah and the other to take the part of the prophets of Baal, King Ahab and the crowd. Arrange the two groups on opposite sides of the room and have either an adult or a confident child reader as the narrator. You will need to practise a few times but the confrontation in the story should come alive.

The story of God passing by in the silence (1 Kings 19:9–18), when practised and performed with sound effects, also communicates very effectively to an audience. The children could practise making a blowing noise for the wind and rustling pieces of cellophane for the fire at the appropriate point in the story; if you are in church, a low pedal note on the organ, or a thunder sheet, would be good for the earthquake.

'God passing by' frieze

> You will need: a long piece of paper, such as lining paper or plain wallpaper cut from a roll (the length will depend on the number of children and the space you have for the display); a variety of different media; prepared Bible verses from the story.

Make it

Prepare the long piece of paper by dividing it into four sections for a frieze. The children could work at this activity all together, or you could divide them into three groups to make pictures depicting wind, earthquake and fire. They could make their pictures using paint, collage or magazine pictures, or images from the internet.

Consider using different techniques for each panel—for instance, chalk and charcoal for wind, sponge painting for the earthquake, and tissue paper for fire. For the final panel, use plain black paper and ask each child to place a small star on it to represent the silence of God. Label each section of the frieze with the relevant Bible verse or phrase.

Chat about it

What would it have been like for Elijah to be in the middle of the wind, earthquake and fire? How do you think he knew that God was not in any of these events, but could only be heard in the silence?

Craft activities

Collage ravens

> You will need: raven shapes drawn on black card (and possibly already cut out) (see template in Appendix 3); black feathers;.PVA glue; gold paper; sequins for eyes.

Make it

Invite the children to glue the feathers on to their raven shapes, finishing them with a gold paper beak and sequin eye.

Chat about it

What kind of food might the ravens have brought Elijah? What other stories do the children remember about God feeding people? (You might remind the children about the manna in the wilderness or the feeding of the 5000.)

Poem: Where is God?

Remind the children how Elijah found God in the silence. Although, in this story, God was not in the wind, or fire or earthquake, there are other stories in the Bible where he appears in these ways. Moses found God in the burning bush, there was an earthquake at the time of the crucifixion, and God came to the disciples at Pentecost in wind and flame. Sometimes the manifestation is gentle and soothing (like Elijah's silence or the dove at Jesus' baptism) and at other times more powerful. Invite the children to think about where they are most likely to find God.

Take them through writing a poem line by line. Brainstorm the many different kinds of fire (candle flame, cooking fire, bonfire, volcano, lightning strike, a single match in the darkness, open fire shared at Christmas with friends, and so on). Ask them to think about the type of fire in which God might manifest himself and give a specific reason for the choice. Begin each line of the poem, 'God is in...' or 'God is where...'. The poem might begin, 'God is in a flow of lava overcoming everything in his way' or 'God is where the light from a single candle shines from a dark window, guiding the lost home.'

For the next line, you might consider in what sort of weather you might find God (sunny spring day, crisp snowy winter, blustery autumn); then in what sort of sound might you find God (clear ringing bell, rhythmic beating drum, deafening dawn chorus); in what sort of scenery (fertile country fields, bustling city streets, the stillness of the arctic night, the loneliness of the ocean, the emptiness of space); and finally among what sort of people might you find God (large crowds at a popular church, a few pensioners in a country church, in a scene of celebration, in a scene of mourning). Add any ideas of your own.

When the children have written these lines, ask them to choose the three or four best lines to form their final poem. You might find it interesting to compare poems and talk about the reasons children have chosen particular images (although no one should be pressured to explain or even share their poem if they do not wish to do so).

If you wanted to make a group compilation poem, pick the best lines as a joint effort to make the best poem you can. You could write it up and put it on display, publish it in your parish magazine and/or use it for prayer.

Flour and salt dough modelling

The widow who looked after Elijah had a constant supply of flour, so you might use modelling dough (made with flour and salt) to create a three-dimensional representation of one of Elijah's stories. If you have lots of children, recreating the scene with the prophets of Baal would work well.

> You will need: playdough (for recipe, see Appendix 2); a wooden board to display the scene (you might like to prepare this by painting it a suitable colour or creating the landscape for the figures to inhabit).

Make it

Remind children of the story you have chosen to represent. Discuss who was there and what needs to be modelled to create the scene. Invite the children to make models to populate the story.

Cooking

Sandwiches

> You will need: hand-washing equipment; preparation boards; sliced bread; spread; sandwich fillings (jam is easy and enjoyable).

Make it

Make sure the children have washed and dried their hands before preparing the food. You may need to demonstrate how to make a sandwich first, but then invite the children to make some sandwiches to serve each other during the break.

Chat about it

Remember how God asked the ravens to look after Elijah by giving him food.

Discussion activities

Voice of God

Talk with the children about what they think the voice of God might be like. How do we hear what God has to say? How do we understand him? If you have a supply of percussion instruments, you might consider asking the children to choose an instrument that they think might sound most like the voice of God, and then ask them why.

Conscience alley

Elijah chose to stand up for his belief and to hold fast to his faith in God, even when it seemed that no one else shared that faith. Think about why he might have been tempted to abandon his faith: he might have had more friends; life would have been easier; he could have joined in celebrations with the worshippers of Baal; he might have been able to get a good job and make a better living. Then discuss the reasons why he chose not to follow that path.

Choose one person to be Elijah (children can take turns at this role). Divide the rest into two groups and line them up so that the children are facing each other, with enough space for 'Elijah' to walk down the line between them. As Elijah walks down the line, children from each side shout advice to him. On one side are tempters trying to persuade Elijah to abandon his faith, while the group on the other side is encouraging him to hold firm.

Prayers

Prayer circle

Link hands to form a circle and remember that we are all linked together because we share the same faith. Remember that there are millions of other people in the world who also share our faith.

Pray for those who serve God in places where they are outnumbered, those who feel alone in their faith, and those who feel that no one will listen to them. Ask God to strengthen their faith and help them to remember that there are people far away who are praying for them. If your church has any particular links with communities in parts of the world where they face these difficulties, add them. The children may have suggestions for places they wish to pray for.

Guided visualisation: Elijah meets God in silence

This story is in 1 Kings 19:9–18. It is quite short and, in many versions, has a poetic quality, so it is worth reading it straight from the Bible. However, you might try this guided visualisation to help the children to think about the story.

Try to sit comfortably—back straight, shoulders relaxed, feet on the floor. Close your eyes and listen to the sounds you can hear around you. Focus first on the sounds you can hear far away: what is the faintest sound? An aeroplane flying overhead, the wind in the trees outside, or birds singing? Listen to the sounds from other parts of the building, perhaps conversations happening in another room. Now try to hear sounds within the room—the hum of the lights, the tick as the hands on the clock move round, the sound of my voice, people sitting nearby shifting slightly. Now listen to the sounds within yourself—the thump of your heart, breath filling and emptying from your lungs, blood rushing through the veins in your ears.

I want you to imagine how Elijah might have felt. You have done what you thought was right, but you feel so alone. You feel that you are the last person left alive who knows and worships God. Imagine how frightening it would be to have to run from people who were trying to harm you. Now here you are alone, crouching, cowering by yourself inside a mountain cave. It is dark and cold.

Imagine the strange, sharp shapes of the mountain that you might see looming out of the dark. Think about the damp, mossy smell of the cave. Think about what you might hear—perhaps the sound of a mountain stream, perhaps the snuffling or pattering of small animals as they brush past you. Feel the grit under your feet and the damp slime on the cave walls.

You begin to notice the wind strengthening. First it whistles past the entrance to the cave, but, as it strengthens, it makes swirls and eddies within your shelter. As the wind gets stronger, it begins to howl through the valleys, making a strange echoing sound among the rocks. It starts to scream past the peaks so strongly that you can hear boulders falling and thudding. You huddle deep inside your cloak and shrink back against the wall.

The wind and rockfalls begin to shake the cave, and you realise that the earth itself is heaving. You steady yourself against the wall and can feel the vibration through the rock. You hear a low roar and rumble as though the mountain itself is being torn apart. The force of creation makes you feel like an insect, powerless to do anything except wait.

As the earthquake fades, another sound reaches you—a crackling like someone walking on dried leaves. As it gets closer, you can hear the spitting fury of a fire. As it catches the twisted trees outside the cave, they blossom into flame as the sap explodes. Fiery fingers reach inside the cave, exploring cracks and crevices, and flames lick around you. You shield your face with your hood and hands, but you can see flickering red through your eyelids and can feel the burning heat with each breath. The blistering smoke takes away your breath as you shrink backwards into a crevice in the walls.

The fire consumes what it can and begins to die down. Rock splinters and clinks as it cools. The soft night air returns and allows you to breathe. The world of sound and sensation recedes. Time seems to slow, as though creation itself is breathing. In the silence you get to your feet, cover your head and go to the entrance of the cave. The darkness is smooth as velvet; there is no cold, no heat. You feel rather than see the vastness of creation above, below and around you, and you feel the hand of God holding you in the right place in that creation. There is no fear, but there is the realisation of the presence of God—solidity without form, voice without sound. Be held there for a moment on the mountain with God.

Feel your own vitality. Listen to the sound of the blood in your ears, air filling and emptying from your lungs, your heart thumping. Now listen to the sounds in the room—the hum of the lights, tick of the clock, the sound of my voice. Now listen to sounds outside and the furthest sound you can possibly hear.

When you're ready, have a good stretch and open your eyes.

The story of Esther

Key Bible focus

Xerxes liked Esther more than he did any of the other young women. None of them pleased him as much as she did, and straight away he fell in love with her and crowned her queen in place of Vashti. In honour of Esther he gave a big dinner for his leaders and officials. Then he declared a holiday everywhere in his kingdom and gave expensive gifts.

ESTHER 2:17–18

The story of Esther has drama, excitement, romance and attempted genocide thwarted by clever planning.

The whole book of Esther is rather long but there is an abridged version below with 'hot-seating' possibilities noted and some examples of questions. To keep things moving, you might want to limit the number of questions that can be asked each time someone occupies the hot seat. If the children are new to hot-seating, you might need to ask an adult to demonstrate the idea first. If you feel it will take too long, you can take out a few of the hot-seat suggestions. The children asking the questions could pretend they are journalists researching their story.

It is worth noting that some Bibles call the king Ahasuerus instead of Xerxes. Don't worry about which name he has, as he is the same person.

- Esther used all her cleverness and influence to protect her people from danger. Can you think of someone else in the Bible who put all his efforts into protecting his people and saving them from danger?

The bravery of Queen Esther

You could either tell the story straight through first before talking about it, or a little bit at a time, using hot-seating between each episode to explore it as you go along. Whoever sits in the hot seat takes on the character from the story: they answer questions as though they were that person. If you wish, they could wear a particular hat (one of a selection of hats). You could either assign one character to each child or the children could take it in turns.

King Xerxes gave a great banquet for all the men in his capital city of Susa. It was held in the palace gardens and it lasted seven days. The wine was served in solid gold cups.

Inside the palace, Queen Vashti was holding a banquet for the women. On the seventh day, the king decided to show off his beautiful queen.

'Bring Queen Vashti here,' he ordered the servants, but the queen refused to come. She made the king look silly in front of all his guests. He was furious.

Hot seat: *Queen Vashti (Questions might include: Why didn't you go to the king when he asked you? What were you doing? What did you expect the king to do when you didn't turn up?)*

King Xerxes sent for his advisers. 'If the other women hear about this,' they told him, 'every wife in the country will think she can disobey her husband.'

There was only one thing to do. 'Send Queen Vashti away,' commanded the king. 'I will have a new queen.'

So the search for a new queen began. All the most beautiful girls in Persia were sent to the palace. For a year they stayed in the king's harem. They were put on a special diet and every day they were massaged with sweet-scented oils. Then the king sent for each of them in turn.

Hot seat: *One of the candidates (Possible questions: What's your name and where are you from? Why do you want to be queen? What personal qualities do you have that will make you a suitable candidate?)*

The most beautiful of them all was Esther, the adopted daughter of Mordecai the Jew. Everyone loved her and, as soon as the king saw her, he chose her to be his queen.

Hot seat: *Esther (Possible questions: What did you feel when Xerxes chose you to be queen? What would you like to do now you are queen? How do you think your life will change?)*

One day Mordecai heard about a plot to kill the king. He told Esther, and the king was very grateful. He wrote Mordecai's name in the official palace records.

Hot seat: *Mordecai*

Some time after this, a man called Haman was made chief of staff to the king. He was proud and vain and cruel. Everyone had to kneel before him. Only Mordecai refused. 'I am a Jew,' he said, 'and my people kneel only to God.'

Hot seat: *Haman*

From that moment, Haman made up his mind to kill Mordecai and all the Jews. He went to the king and said, 'There is a nation in your kingdom that refuses to obey your laws. Let me have them destroyed.'

The king gave Haman the ring that he used as a royal seal and Haman sent orders, sealed with the king's ring, to the governors of all the provinces, telling them to kill the Jews on a certain day.

No one at the palace knew that Queen Esther was a Jewish girl.

Hot seat: *Esther*

Mordecai and all the Jews went into mourning. They ate no food and they wept out loud. 'Whatever is wrong?' Esther asked, and Mordecai told her. 'Go to the king and plead for the lives of your people,' he said.

'It's a month since the king sent for me,' Esther replied, 'and if I go to him without being asked, he may have me killed.'

'But God may have made you queen in order to save us all,' said Mordecai. 'No one else can speak to the king for us.'

So Esther went to the king. Haman was with him—but the king was glad to see her. Esther waited until the moment was right. She invited them both to dinner that night and it went well. 'Come back again tomorrow,' she said.

Hot seat: *Haman*

Haman was flattered. Dinner alone with the king and queen! But the thought of Mordecai spoilt everything, so he ordered his men to build a gallows, ready to hang the Jew the next day.

That night, the king could not sleep. He sat up, reading through the palace records—and there was Mordecai's name.

Hot seat: *King Xerxes*

'I must reward Mordecai,' thought the king. So, instead of being hanged, as Haman had planned, Mordecai was given royal honours.

The next night at dinner, the king thought how lovely his queen was looking. 'I will give you anything you want,' he said to her. 'You have only to ask.'

Hot seat: *Esther*

'I and all my people are to be killed,' Esther answered. 'I ask for my life and the lives of my people.'

Hot seat: *King Xerxes*

The king turned pale. 'Who is responsible for this?' he asked. 'Haman,' Esther answered. 'He had a gallows made, ready to hang Mordecai,' one of the servants added. 'Then hang him on his own gallows,' said the king, and that was what they did.

Esther saved the lives of all her people that night, and the king made Mordecai his new chief of staff.

Displays for the church

Because the story of Esther has such dramatic possibilities, the children might like to present it as a drama to the wider congregation. They could perform it as a play or, if you have only a few children, they might use sock puppets (see the craft section) and present a puppet show.

If you'd prefer a static display, you might try making a large crown.

Esther's crown

You will need: large sheets of gold card; glue; stapler; coloured paper; cellophane; black felt-tip marker.

Make it

Cut out crown-shaped strips from the card and staple the ends together to make a large crown. Use the coloured paper to cut large jewel shapes: you may need to mark these on the paper first, to get accurate shapes.

Discuss the qualities that Esther possessed, and what she did to save her people. Invite the children to write down these qualities and actions using black marker pen on the jewel shapes. To obtain a shiny finish, glue cellophane over the jewel shapes before sticking them on to the crown.

Chat about it

Discuss with the children Esther's personal qualities, which enabled her to be so brave. How did her actions help her people? Was she a good queen?

Craft activities

Making TVs

You will need: shoeboxes; cardboard kitchen roll tubes (two for each shoebox); tracing paper; scissors; felt-tip pens; sticky tape.

Make it

This activity takes a bit of preparation and is fairly lengthy, but worth it. Children could make one TV each or work in pairs.

Cut a screen-shaped hole in the bottom of the shoebox. Then

cut enough circular holes to slide the cardboard tubes through either side of the 'screen'. Cut sheets of tracing paper for as many screens as are required (three, perhaps), with extra for the paper to be attached to the kitchen roll at the beginning and end of the picture sequence. Mark the three (or more if required) screens in pencil on to the paper and ask each child to draw and colour pictures illustrating the story (in the correct order) using felt-tip pens. If you have some templates, it would be easy for the children to trace round the shapes if they wish.

When the pictures are finished, attach one end of the tracing paper strip to the right-hand tube (as you look at the screen) and the other end to the left-hand tube. Roll the tracing paper round the left-hand tube and adjust so that the first picture is showing. Rotate the right-hand tube so that the first picture wraps round the kitchen roll and the second appears in the screen.

If you leave the lid off the shoebox, it will enable light to shine through the tracing paper, to make it translucent and more like a television.

Chat about it

This activity takes quite a bit of concentration, but further exploration of the story should be possible while the children are working.

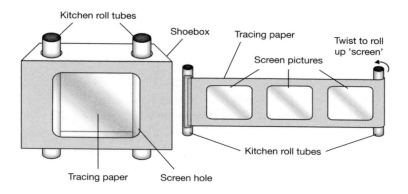

If making TVs is too time-consuming or needs too much preparation, the children could make storyboards or a comic strip of the story.

Sock puppets

> You will need: socks; glue; fabric and felt scraps; wool.

Make it

Show the children how, by tucking the toe in and back towards the heel, a sock can be used to make a puppet. You could show the children a finished puppet to help them understand how it will work.

Invite the children to use the fabric and felt scraps and wool to glue on the features for their puppets—hair, eyes, and so on. Allow them to dry. Children could choose two characters from the story to make. If required, you could use the puppets to present the story as a puppet show.

Chat about it

How can we make the characters distinctive so that we can tell who they are? What might these people have looked like?

Cooking

Making sweets

Esther gave her dinner party to make sure King Xerxes was in a good mood. Some delicious sweets might well have done the trick.

> You will need: icing sugar; milk; peppermint essence; food colouring (optional); chocolate (optional); work surface; mixing bowl; rolling-pins; weighing scales.

Make it

Peppermint creams are easy and don't require cooking. You will need to mix about 25ml milk with about 250g icing sugar to make a stiff paste (hands are the best tool for doing this). If you mix a little food colouring (optional) and a little peppermint essence with the milk first, an even distribution of flavour and colour will be easier to achieve. If you want to be really adventurous, you can melt chocolate in a microwave and dip the sweets in it. Put the peppermint creams in attractive boxes for the children to take home.

If you have basic cooking facilities, you might try making fairy cakes instead, following the basic recipe in the chapter on Abraham. Add a little jam on top of each cake before baking. This ends up as a jam filling as the cake mixture rises around the jam, and might make the cakes seem more royal.

Games

Hangman

You will need: paper and pens or pencils.

Play the game in the usual way, with one child thinking of a word and writing dashes for each letter, and the others guessing what the letters are. Each correct guess gives a letter in the word, and each incorrect guess produces a line in the gallows.

Discussion activities

If you used the 'hot-seating' version of the story, this should have provoked plenty of discussion. Hot seating while you're working through the story, when the children don't know the outcome, may well produce some interesting questions and answers. However, if you told the story without embellishments, a hot-seating session afterwards would work too.

Prayers

Newspaper prayers

Use a newspaper or papers to find people or situations that need our prayers. Look particularly for national or international stories. If you wish, you could cut these stories out of the paper and, as you say each prayer, place them on the altar or in a bowl to represent offering the situations to God.

Pray especially for people who have power over others—people who govern and make decisions that affect all of us. Pray for foreign leaders as well as our own. Pray that God will help them to make the right choices.

Stories of Old Testament prophets: Daniel, Isaiah, Jeremiah, Ezekiel

Key Bible focus

Suddenly the king jumped up and shouted, 'Weren't only three men tied up and thrown into the fire?' 'Yes, Your Majesty,' the people answered. 'But I see four men walking around in the fire,' the king replied. 'None of them is tied up or harmed, and the fourth one looks like a god.' Nebuchadnezzar went closer to the flaming furnace and said to the three young men, 'You servants of the Most High God, come out at once!'

DANIEL 3:24–26

The books of these major prophets are long and contain much that is not easily accessible for children. However, there are episodes or short passages that are rich in inspiration for them. Stories in the book of Daniel offer danger, infernos, wild animals and mysterious supernatural communication. The books of Isaiah, Jeremiah and Ezekiel also offer some meaningful and memorable images that can be explored.

These men all understood that God would send a Messiah to bring everyone close to him. Although they lived and died many years before Jesus was born, they encouraged the people to watch for the fulfilment of God's promise and their words described him in advance. We read their words today as a reminder that Jesus is the fulfilment of God's plan.

- The Old Testament prophets spoke and acted for God. Can you think of someone else in the Bible who spoke and acted for God, even when people didn't want to hear?

There are three stories in the book of Daniel that will provide plenty of excitement for children.

- Printed below is a version of the story of the fiery furnace with some audience participation (Daniel 3).
- The story of the writing on the wall (Daniel 5) could be told with special effects, using a PowerPoint presentation (or a hidden typist) and a projector.
- Many children's storybooks feature Daniel in the lions' den (Daniel 6).

As far as the other prophets are concerned, you might consider looking at:

- Jeremiah's image of God as the potter fashioning his creation (Jeremiah 18:1–6).
- Isaiah's words reminding us that God calls us by name (Isaiah 43:1–7).
- Isaiah's words about preparing the way for Christ, famously set to music by G.F. Handel in *Messiah* (Isaiah 40:3–5).
- Ezekiel's vision of the dry bones (Ezekiel 37:1–14).

All these passages are short and could be read directly from a children's Bible.

Daniel's friends in the fiery furnace

Try telling this story with some audience participation. Practise the responses below to certain words (shown in bold text).

• **Shadrach**	'One'
• **Meshach**	'Two'
• **Abednego**	'Three'
• **King**	'Nebuchadnezzar'
• **Bow down**	Bow

- **Worship**   Hands in praying position
- **Flaming furnace**   'Ouch'
- **The Most High God** 'Hurrah'

King Nebuchadnezzar ordered a huge golden statue to be built and he commanded his officials to come from everywhere in his kingdom to the dedication of the statue.

The **king** commanded that, when the music played, everyone must **bow down** and **worship** the statue. Anyone who refused would at once be thrown into a **flaming furnace**.

So as soon as the people heard the music, they **bowed down** and **worshipped** the golden statue that **King** Nebuchadnezzar had set up.

Some Babylonians used this as a chance to get the Jews into trouble with **King** Nebuchadnezzar. They told the **king** that three Jewish men, called **Shadrach**, **Meshach** and **Abednego**, had refused to **bow down** and **worship** the **king**'s gods and his statue.

King Nebuchadnezzar was furious, so he sent for **Shadrach**, **Meshach** and **Abednego**, and said, 'I hear that you refuse to **bow down** and **worship** my gods and the golden statue I have set up. Now I am going to give you one more chance. If you **bow down** and **worship** the statue when you hear the music, everything will be all right. But if you don't, you will at once be thrown into a **flaming furnace**. No god can save you from me.'

The three men replied, '**King** Nebuchadnezzar, we don't need to defend ourselves. The **Most High God** we **worship** can save us from you and your **flaming furnace**. But even if he doesn't, we still won't **bow down** and **worship** your gods and the golden statue you have set up.'

The **king**'s face twisted with anger and he ordered the **flaming furnace** to be heated seven times hotter than usual. He commanded some of his strongest soldiers to tie up **Shadrach, Meshach** and **Abednego** and to throw them into the **flaming furnace**.

Shadrach, Meshach and **Abednego** were thrown into the **flaming furnace** with all their clothes still on. The **flaming furnace** was so hot that the flames leaped out and killed the soldiers who were putting the men into it.

Suddenly **King** Nebuchadnezzar jumped up and shouted, 'Weren't only three men tied up and thrown into the **flaming furnace**?'

'Yes, Your Majesty,' the people answered.

'But I see four men walking around inside the fire,' the **king** replied. 'None of them is tied up or harmed and the fourth looks like a god.'

King Nebuchadnezzar went closer to the **flaming furnace** and said to **Shadrach, Meshach** and **Abednego**, 'You servants of the **Most High God**, come out at once!'

Shadrach, Meshach and **Abednego** came out. They were not burnt, their hair wasn't scorched, and their clothes didn't even smell of smoke. **King** Nebuchadnezzar said, 'Praise the **Most High God** for sending an angel to rescue his servants! They trusted the **Most High God** and refused to obey my commands. Yes, they chose to die rather than to **worship** or serve any god except their own. And I won't allow people of any nation or race to say anything against the **Most High God**.'

Displays for the church

Handprint faith display

We are very fortunate to be able to worship God without fear of punishment, so why not create a handprint display?

You will need: a large sheet of card; brightly coloured water-based paint such as poster paint; paintbrushes; black marker pen; hand-washing equipment.

Make it

Invite each child to write a statement of faith in black marker pen on the sheet of card. The children should choose what they want to write and should not be forced or over-persuaded to write anything. Using poster paint (different bright colours will be most effective), invite them to make a handprint over their statement. Depending on the thickness and transparency of the paint, you may need to touch up the words when the paint has dried.

Craft activities

Furnace spinner

This activity requires quite a lot of preparation, but the finished product is a picture with a fiery coloured circle at the back. When this is spun round, it looks as though the flames are flickering.

You will need: cellophane or tissue paper in different flame colours; sheets of acetate; stiff black card (A4 size); black paper; flame-coloured metallic and/or holographic paper; paper fasteners.

Make it

It is worth working through this activity in advance of your session, to make sure you understand how it fits together and so that you can show the children what the finished product will look like.

First, prepare the stiff black card, which will be the front of the picture. Trim about half an inch from one long side. With a pair of compasses, mark and cut out a circular aperture towards the top of the card. Then cut a circle of acetate a little bigger than the aperture, and glue it over the back of the aperture to make a circular window. Find the centre of the acetate window and make a hole there for the paper fastener.

Next, cut out four figures from the black paper (see template in Appendix 3) for each picture. The children will arrange and glue these over the acetate window. You will also need to cut out flame shapes using coloured metallic and/or holographic paper. The flame shapes can be placed round the bottom edge of the aperture and acetate window.

To make the wheel that fits behind, you will need to cut some card washers to allow the wheel to move freely and another circle of acetate: this must be large enough to allow it to protrude over the edges of the black card, so that it can be spun round. Cut some circles of flame-coloured cellophane or tissue paper and then cut them into six segments. The children can glue the coloured tissue or cellophane on to the spinning circle of acetate.

Assemble the picture by inserting a paper fastener through the acetate window, the washer behind, the cellophane-covered acetate spinner at the back and the final washer.

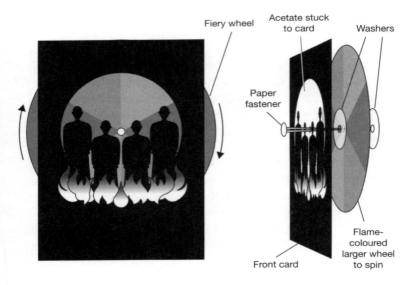

Chat about it

Talk about the story of the fiery furnace. What might it have been like to meet God in the flames, and to be inside the fire but not burnt? (You may need to add a 'Don't try this at home' caveat.)

Collage lion masks

You will need: lion mask shapes; collage materials such as wool and felt; glue; sticks or elastic; staples.

Make it

Provide each child with a mask shape (see template in Appendix 3). Set out the collage materials on the table, making sure you have material that will be useful for decorating lions, such as appropriately coloured wool and felt. Invite the children to make their own lion masks. The masks can either be mounted on sticks, to be held in front of the face, or elastic can be stapled to each side so that the mask fits round the child's head.

Chat about it

Talk about what the night in the lion pit might have been like, for both Daniel and King Darius.

My name

This activity ties in well with Isaiah's words about God calling each of us by name (Isaiah 43:1–7).

You will need: coloured card or thick paper; pens and/or paint and brushes (or any other media you think the children would enjoy); baby names book; selection of different types of lettering (perhaps a calligraphy book) for the children to look at.

If you have access to computers, you could use them to carry out this activity. Older children especially are likely to be proficient in choosing and altering fonts, colours and backgrounds using any generally available software.

Make it

Talk about the meanings of the names of the children in your group. They may have interesting stories to tell about why they were given their names, or you could look up the names in the baby names book to check what they mean.

Talk about the importance of our names and why we have them. Discuss how our name gives us an identity: a surname or family name denotes who we belong to, and a Christian name or first name really becomes a part of who we are. Lots of people are named after relatives who have had the same name, or famous saints, and some children are given names like Grace or Faith in the hope that they might grow up to have these characteristics.

Look at different ways of writing letters and how they affect the way a word looks: different types of lettering have a different feeling to them.

Invite the children to create a picture based on their name. They can choose what sort of lettering and colours to use, and they might also illuminate each letter in a way that is appropriate to themselves.

Chat about it

Do our names always suit us? Do we live up to our names? Do you wish you had a different name and, if so, what would it be?

Jeremiah's pots

You will need: clay (you could use air-drying clay or salt dough that needs baking—but remember to send instructions home about how to do this); pictures of different pots, showing a variety of shapes (optional).

Make it

Invite the children to make their own pots using whatever shape they like. They might try to make a shape that is impractical for the materials you have. If this happens, remind them of the story of Jeremiah: just like the potter, they can change their minds and make a shape more suited to the clay they have.

Chat about it

Talk about what sort of pot the children are trying to make, and why. What will they use their pot for? (Unless you have really professional supplies and, probably, the help of a professional potter, make sure the children know that they won't be able to use their pottery to eat or drink from.) How easy is it to make a perfect pot? If you were a piece of pottery, what sort might you be: a delicate bone china cup, rarely used but beautiful, or a well-loved but chipped teapot, or perhaps an elegant vase that is always filled with flowers?

Isaiah's civil engineering

> You will need: a patch of garden or churchyard (or a large tray filled with sand and toy dumper trucks); hand trowels and forks; hand-washing equipment.

Make it

Look at the passage in Isaiah about making a straight way for the Lord (Isaiah 40:3–5). It talks about preparing the way for the Messiah. Filling in valleys and flattening mountains and hills isn't an easy task!

Invite the children to prepare a small patch of garden or churchyard, ready for planting some bulbs or bedding plants. Encourage them to fork the soil over, perhaps adding some compost, and get rid of any weeds. Check for stinging nettles or thorny plants before the children get stuck into this task.

If you have no garden, or if you think the children would enjoy it more, pile up some damp sand in a large tray (or use a sandpit). Ask the children to use the toy dumper trucks to construct a road through the sand hill, but they can only use the scoops on the trucks to move sand. Remind them that the road needs to be level and smooth.

Chat about it

How hard is this work? What do you think Isaiah meant about making a straight way? Explore the metaphor of roads and, perhaps, bridges too.

Blow-by-blow painting

You will need: runny paint; drinking straws; large sheets of thick paper; spoons or brushes.

Make it

Give each child a sheet of paper and a drinking straw. Explain that they will be doing some painting but that, instead of using brushes, they need to blow the paint where they want it to go. Demonstrate how to drop some paint on the paper (use a spoon or brush) and then use the straw to blow it to make a line. Make sure you explain that the straw shouldn't touch the paint, and the children should blow, never suck!

Invite the children to make their own pictures using different colours. They may find it easier sometimes to turn the paper, not the straw or themselves, to change direction. When they've had a chance to practise, you might want to challenge them to draw a person or an animal to see how well they can control the paint.

Chat about it

Remind the children of Ezekiel's vision and how God breathed life into the bones.

Games

Musical statues

Use the usual rules to play musical statues. Remember the part that music played in the story of the flaming furnace: when King Nebuchadnezzar's music started, everyone had to worship him.

Lions game

Ask the children to stand in a circle. One child stands in the centre of the circle as 'Daniel'. The object of the game is for the children on the edge to creep towards Daniel, and the first to touch him wins the game. However, they can only move when Daniel can't see them. If he spots anyone moving, they must move back to the edge of the circle.

Ezekiel's bones

> You will need: pictures of skeletons cut into pieces (for younger children you will need to use fewer pieces and keep groups of bones together; for experts in human anatomy you could disarticulate each metatarsal).

To avoid frustration, you may wish to pack the pieces for each complete skeleton jigsaw into its own envelope.

Play it

Invite the children to put the jigsaws together. Who can complete their jigsaw first? Can the children name any of the bones?

Prayers

Pray by a window

Try praying by a window as Daniel did. If your room has a low-level window that will open, so much the better. Otherwise you might try praying by the open door.

Pray particularly for anyone who is afraid and needs to find courage to deal with their situation. Perhaps you could include children who are bullied or ill-treated but afraid to speak out, or people who are afraid to admit they are Christians.

Breathing prayer

Remember how God breathed life into the dry bones in Ezekiel's vision. Talk to the children about the word 'inspiration': it literally means 'breathing in'. Invite the children to think about how they might breathe in God's inspiration; then, in a few moments of quiet, ask everyone to think their own prayer with every in-breath they take. Try to encourage the children to breathe quietly and normally so as not to disturb anyone else.

This activity will not suit all groups: you will know your own group well enough to decide whether or not they'll be able to cope with this prayer idea. It may just produce fits of the giggles.

The story of John the Baptist

Key Bible focus

John said, 'I am just baptising with water. But someone more powerful is going to come, and I am not good enough even to untie his sandals. He will baptise you with the Holy Spirit and with fire.'

LUKE 3:16

John the Baptist provides the bridge between the Old and New Testaments: he was the last of the prophets and one of the first people to recognise Jesus as the Christ. There isn't a great deal of detail about him in the Gospels, but what we are told is colourful and intriguing, from his ascetic way of life to the gruesome and bizarre manner of his death. The story of John baptising Jesus is perhaps the obvious one to tell the children, since it marks the start of Jesus' ministry. The story of John's birth and naming in Luke's Gospel is a good way to tie in John with his role as the great last prophet, preparing the way for Jesus. The story of his beheading at the instigation of Salome is also likely to fascinate children, but perhaps as a footnote.

The Gospel of Luke contains the most detail about John the Baptist. The story of his birth is in Luke 1 and Luke 2; the baptism of Jesus is in Luke 3:15–22. The story of the death of John the Baptist is told in Matthew 14:1–12, with a more detailed version in Mark 6:17–29.

* John spent his ministry preparing people for Jesus. How could we make ourselves ready for Jesus?

Displays for the church

Waterfall banner

> You will need: a prepared fabric banner, hemmed on all sides, with casing for a pole at the top or some other means of hanging it; strips of different blue fabrics and ribbons to make a waterfall effect; sponges (the sponge sides of rectangular pan scourers are good for this and can make angular rock shapes); fabric paint in grey, brown and green; glue; appliqué letters and/or fabric pen for lettering.

Make it

Invite the children to use sponges and grey, brown and green paint to create a rocky effect down each side of the banner, then glue the blue fabric strips and ribbon between the rocks to create a waterfall effect. The strips can be twisted and looped as they are stuck to the banner to make the waterfall look lively and give it some texture. You could even add some white tuile fabric for a foamy effect. You could end the waterfall in a painted or fabric pool at the bottom of the banner. Add a suitable Bible verse at the bottom, such as, 'The water I give is like a flowing fountain that gives eternal life' (John 4:14).

This banner also looks good with the word 'WELCOME' in appliqué letters down one side of the waterfall, which would make it appropriate to be hung at the entrance to your church.

Chat about it

Waterfalls carve a path through a landscape, just as John set out to make a path for Jesus. You could talk about this or, if geography has no appeal, use the opportunity to talk about how John used water to baptise people, as a ritual cleansing to prepare them to hear and believe Jesus. What sort of cleansing was required? Do we have to have a bath before coming to church or do we mean some other sort of 'clean'? How can we make ourselves 'clean' for God?

Craft activities

Sandals

> You will need: two layers of thick corrugated card cut into sole shapes (one with the lines running lengthways, the other widthways); strips of card to make the 'uppers' (these need to be flexible, but also able to keep a loop shape, so bendy card is likely to be ideal); scissors; glue.

Make it

Show the children some pictures of Roman-type sandals, which the people of Jesus' time might have worn. Invite them to try designing and making their own sandal by folding the ends of the card strips over and sticking them to the top side of the sole. The children could make their designs more exciting by cutting slots in a lengthways strip in order to weave crossways strips through. If you want to neaten up the sandal, a card shape could be stuck inside to hide the ends of the strips.

Top

Side

Central tongue: crosspieces woven through

Chat about it

Sandals like these would have been worn in New Testament times. What might it have been like to wear them? What would the advantages or disadvantages have been? What might it be like to walk in the footprints of John the Baptist or Jesus?

Writing tablets

You will need: pliable modelling material such as playdough or clay (you need to be able to roll it out like pastry); rolling-pins; sharpened pieces of dowel or blunt pencils. If you have them, you could use old picture frames (without the glass) to contain the material and give a more realistic tablet effect.

Make it

Give each child a lump of the modelling material and a rolling-pin (or one between two). Show them how to roll out the material to an even depth and write on it with the dowel or blunt pencil. Show them how the marks can then be flattened out using fingers or the end of the rolling-pin so that the surface is smooth again. Try to dissuade them from re-rolling, as their tablet will get too thin. Invite the children to have a go.

Chat about it

Talk about how people in biblical times often used 'tablets' to write on. These weren't electronic like ours, but were sheets of clay or wax in a wooden frame. Their equivalent of paper was very expensive, so these tablets were used as a cheap alternative. Children were often taught to write using them, or people would write reminders for themselves. Zechariah used a tablet to tell people what John's name would be.

What do you think it would be like to be able to communicate only using one of these tablets?

Play it

To extend the experience, prepare a series of cards and invite the children to take turns to communicate the idea on the card using only the tablet. Older children might, for instance, try to describe the plot of a book or a news event. If the children are younger (or you have insufficient time) ask them to communicate an idea or object by drawing on the tablet.

If you didn't want to make tablets, you could use a game of charades to illustrate how difficult it can be to communicate without being able to speak.

Sackcloth painting

> You will need: sacking or hessian fabric already glued on to thick card; brushes; plenty of acrylic paint; water.

Make it

Give each child a hessian-covered board and invite them to use the paint to create their own picture. They might want to illustrate the story of Jesus' baptism or create a picture of some water (a river, the sea or a lake), or they might choose to paint the dove. As the surface is rough, they are likely to use plenty of paint. Encourage them not to use a plastering technique, but to allow the texture of the fabric to show.

Chat about it

Talk about the story and, if you wish, about John's chosen attire. Why might John have dressed like this? How might people today show devotion to God in the way they dress or show how they feel about something (such as a protest movement or a rock band)?

Water painting

Make it

Show how you can paint with plain water and then, gently and sparingly, sprinkle powder paint over the wet paper. Look at how the paint dissolves and forms patterns.

You may need to experiment first in order to get the quantities of water and paint right. Allow the children to try it out before using the technique to create patterns or a picture.

Chat about it

Just as this technique can produce some surprising and interesting results, the way that God prepares for each one of us can turn out to be unexpected.

Doves

Make it

Give each child a dove shape and ask them to decorate the doves in whatever way they wish, making sure they keep the wing slot free. When this is done, make a concertina fold with the paper you have chosen for the wings, and thread the folded paper through the wing slot. Open the folds out on either side to make wings.

If you wish, punch holes in the doves and put thread through so that they can be hung from the ceiling. For the wings, paper that has different colours on each side can be very effective.

Chat about it

Talk with the children about why they think the Holy Spirit was 'like a dove'. In what ways might they be similar?

Cooking

Honey sandwiches

As with any food-related activity, you will need to check whether any of the children have food allergies. It is not recommended for babies under one year to have honey.

> You will need: sliced bread; butter or spread; honey; knife; plates.

Make it

Show the children how to make honey sandwiches and supervise them as they have a go. Pile the sandwiches on to a plate and invite the children to offer them to everyone as a snack at break time.

Chat about it

Do the children like honey? How tasty do they think their honey sandwiches are? Remind them that John the Baptist ate honey but he would have needed to find it himself from wild bees, which might not have been keen to share it with him. How would they feel about having to eat honey all the time?

You could also talk about eating locusts: some insects are considered delicacies in some parts of the world. How would the children feel about eating locusts? We don't know whether John did this, but might they have tasted better with honey on them?

Games

Quick-on-the-draw memory game

You will need: items from the story of John the Baptist, such as sand, rock, sandal, honey, picture of a locust, water, feather, sackcloth; tray; tea towel; paper and pencils.

Play it

Prepare a tray with all the items arranged on it and cover it with a tea towel. Give each child paper and a pencil. Remove the tea towel and invite them to spend two minutes looking at the tray and memorising the objects. Then remove the tray from sight or cover it and ask the children to draw the tray from memory. You could offer a small prize for the most accurate and best-executed drawing.

Locust pairs

You will need: pairs of pictures of insects, printed on card and cut into playing card size. If you have access to a computer and printer, clip art or an internet search is likely to provide some good pictures. Include a locust, but only a single one.

Play it

Make sure the cards are shuffled, then lay them out on a table face down in a grid pattern. Invite children to take turns to turn two cards over. If the two cards match, the child keeps them. If they do not, they must be turned face down again and the next child has a go. The object of the game is to collect pairs. If a child turns over the locust card, they miss the next go. The winner is the child with the most pairs. The single locust should be left at the end.

Discussion activity

Baptism of Jesus told with textures

You will need: sand; rough scratchy cloth (for example, sacking); water; feathers.

Try telling the story using different textures. Do this without a book if you can and invite discussion, particularly at the beginning, about the setting of the story.

As an introduction, allow the children to spend some time feeling the texture of dry sand in their fingers while you talk together about the desert and what sort of place it is. You could then move on to talking about the sort of person John the Baptist was and give them some very scratchy, rough cloth, like sacking or hessian, for them to feel. Talk about why John might have wanted to wear such fabric and what it tells us about him. When you begin to tell the children about how John baptised Jesus, allow the children to dip their hands in some water. You might want to tell this part of the story around the font or a large bowl of water. When you describe how the Holy Spirit descended like a dove, give the children some soft feathers to feel and look at.

When you've finished the story, talk about how the different textures help us to understand the story. What contrasting textures were there?

Prayers

Water blessings

Use a large bowl and some water to help the children pray. If you wished, you might pray round the font. Talk to the children about how John used water to baptise Jesus and how baptism is still an important part of church life. Discuss what the water symbolises—

not just ritual cleaning but also an essential support to life, available to rich and poor, people and animals alike. What would the world be like without water?

In the prayers, you might give thanks for our baptism if children in your group have been baptised. You could ask God to help us be ready for Jesus to enter our lives, to make us open enough to hear his teaching. The children might also list the things they have to be grateful for; you can then either include them in a general prayer or invite each child to say a short 'thank you' in turn. With each line of the prayer, add a little water to the bowl or font. When the prayer is finished, say a few words to gather everyone's prayers together. Then invite the children in turn to dip their fingers into the water. If they wish, they could dab the water on their foreheads or draw a cross shape.

Guided visualisation: John the Baptist in the desert

The environment in which John lived and preached is very foreign to us, so try this visualisation with the children to help them think about what it might have been like. Read the text softly, allowing plenty of pauses for the children's imaginations to work. You may need to adapt the details about the place where you are, at the beginning and end of the visualisation. The children may take a little while to settle, and it may take a few attempts at this sort of activity for them to get the hang of stillness.

Try to sit comfortably: back straight, shoulders relaxed, feet on the floor. Close your eyes and think about the wonderful planet we live on, with the great variety of habitat and life—oceans, deserts, mountains, forests, wastelands and farmlands. Think of our place in the world, in Europe, the islands of Great Britain, this country, our town. Think of the communities that make up our town—the shops, the organisations, our own church. Think of the building where we are now. Think of where you are in relation to the walls. Think how high the ceiling is above you. Feel the hardness of the floor beneath you.

I want to transport you to another place and another time. It's a hot, dusty country, nearly 2000 years ago. Imagine you are walking the wilderness of John the Baptist.

Imagine a night spent there in the open. Imagine the feel of the rough, rocky ground digging into your back as you stare up at the night sky, littered with thousands upon thousands of clear bright stars stretching across space. Listen to the scuttling of night creatures that you can't see—though you might be able to sense larger animals passing nearby. Feel the bitter chill of the night air as you shiver, wrapped in a large heavy blanket or cloak.

As day dawns, the rocks around you fade into infinite shades of grey as definition grows and the sky shows a pearly tint. Creatures of the wilderness forage for food or seek shelter before the heat of the day. You may need to catch what insects you can now for food during the day.

You get up, unrested, from the stony ground and begin to walk for warmth. As the sun rises, the mountains in the distance begin to glow with the pinks and yellows of sunrise and the sun begins to warm your cold bones. You have basic leather sandals on your feet but you can feel the uneven rocky surface through them. The ways in the wilderness are uncertain, so you may often stumble and stones will get inside your shoes. The path might be steep and slippery; you may have to climb mountains or descend them. There are a few scrubby plants that you might cling to, but the thorns on some of them could cut your hands.

As the sun rises further into the sky, you have to take off your blanket or cloak to cool down. The sun reflects off the mountains, which now appear in shades of purple and brown in the distance. Exposed skin burns and blisters. You need to find water. Imagine how thirsty you are and how hungry. Animal life has now disappeared. Everything living is sheltering out of the sun, except you. Hear the silence around you: the only sound might be the slipping of your feet or the wind rattling a tree.

Think about why you are here. You know that God is in all places. Here, where you have nothing to distract you, where you are unburdened by possessions, where there is silence, here you may find God more easily. Think about what you might say to God, and what God might say to you in this wilderness.

Now you need to come back to our room in our time. Feel the hardness of the floor; remember the position of the walls and ceiling of the room. Instead of the silence of the first century AD, you can hear sounds of our busy 21st-century life and you need to take your place within it again.

When you are ready, have a good stretch and open your eyes.

The story of Jesus the hero

Key Bible focus

Finally, the devil took Jesus up on a very high mountain and showed him all the kingdoms on earth and their power. The devil said to him, 'I will give all this to you, if you will bow down and worship me.' Jesus answered, 'Go away Satan! The Scriptures say: "Worship the Lord your God and serve only him."' Then the devil left Jesus, and angels came to help him.

MATTHEW 4:8–11

Having looked at a series of Bible heroes, it is fruitful to consider Jesus in the light of the people in the Bible who went before him. How does he compare? Explore with the children the ways in which Jesus is a very unconventional hero.

There are plenty of Bible stories featuring Jesus to choose from, but a story showing an unexpected type of heroism, such as the garden of Gethsemane or the temptation in the wilderness, would be good for this session. You could show an extract from a film such as *Miracle Maker* or use a technique such as Godly Play. If the children know the story well, after a brief refresher ask them to tell you the story or turn it into a play to perform to the congregation. Both these suggested Bible stories are short enough to be read direct from a Bible. You will find the temptation in the wilderness in Matthew 4:1–11 and Luke 4:1–13. The garden of Gethsemane can be found in Matthew 26:36–56 and Mark 14:32–50.

Displays for the church

These display ideas work well if you are using this session, or this group of New Testament sessions, as the culmination of a series on other Bible heroes.

Jesse tree

> You will need: a twiggy branch, or some other type of display 'tree'; gold spray paint (optional); large flowerpot; sand or gravel; circles cut from white card; thread; hole punch; art materials.

Make it

If you wish, you could paint the branch gold in advance of the session. The branch needs to be 'planted' in the pot and held secure using the sand or gravel.

Give each child a card circle and invite them to illustrate the story of one of the Bible heroes they have heard about in previous weeks on their circle. The illustration does not have to be too complicated: a symbol, such as a harp for David or a lion for Daniel, is very effective. You will probably need to agree, before work starts, who will illustrate which hero, and children might need help to decide how to illustrate their hero.

You could use simple colouring pencils or more adventurous media, such as acrylic paint or collage. As the circles are to be hung from the 'tree', both sides of the circle need to be covered.

To assemble the Jesse tree, use the hole punch (or a needle) and string each circle on to a piece of thread. The circles can be hung, like Christmas baubles, from the tree. The top circle should illustrate Jesus.

Chat about it

This activity gives an opportunity to discuss an overview of the previous sessions. You might compare different Bible heroes and talk about how each one dealt with their circumstances differently, or you might talk about ways in which they are similar to each other, or ways in which they are similar to or different from Jesus. How were these Bible heroes part of God's plan leading to the birth of Jesus? Could we ourselves fit on to a post-Jesus Jesse tree?

Jesse cross

This activity is similar, but offers a different way of displaying the children's art.

> You will need: cardboard boxes in good condition and all the same size (half-case of wine size works well); strong glue; paste; masking tape; newspaper; good-quality paper cut to the size of the box faces; art materials.

Make it

In order to give the cross structure time to dry, you will need to prepare it in advance. Re-seal the boxes, then stack them together to form a cross shape and glue them using strong glue (the sort that is left until touch-dry and then makes an instant bond is good). You may need to wait for the vertical part to dry before adding the horizontal arms.

Stick masking tape over the joints to smooth them out, then paste newspaper over the cross for both strength and smoothness. You could paint it with emulsion if you want to be sure of covering up the newsprint. You will probably need to glue the cross on to a platform of thick corrugated card or wood, or a larger box at the base to give it some stability.

Show the children the cardboard box cross and explain that they will be covering it with artwork. If you have painted the cross, and the children are confident artists, they could work directly on to the cross. Otherwise, as with the Jesse tree, invite them to create their designs to reflect different Bible heroes on the pre-cut paper. The artwork can then be glued to the different faces of the cross.

If you are running the session without looking at a series of Bible heroes first, the children could assemble the cross themselves and omit the artwork. A cross covered with newspaper has its own symbolism.

Chat about it

As in the Jesse tree activity, you could talk about Bible heroes in different ways, although the emphasis, if you are using the cross, would be on how the Bible heroes prepared the way for Jesus' death and resurrection.

If the children are making the cross without the artwork, you could talk about how Jesus can be a hero for our world today. How is he different from or similar to the type of hero we might read about in newspapers?

Craft activities

Bookmarks

> You will need: pressed flowers and leaves; glue; ready-cut card bookmarks; laminator; laminating pouches; embroidery thread to make tassels; an example already made.

Make it

Show the children a bookmark that you have already made and laminated. Then invite them to use the pressed flowers and leaves to make their own designs on the bookmarks and glue them in place. The children could write either a Bible verse or a sentence about what Jesus means to them on the back.

Place the bookmarks in laminating pouches, making sure there is sufficient space between them to enable them to be separated later, and laminate them. Cut the laminated pouches to separate the bookmarks.

If you wish, holes can be punched in one end and tassels attached using the embroidery thread.

Chat about it

Talk about where we can find out about Bible heroes. Perhaps the children could use these bookmarks when they are reading more about their favourite heroes in their own Bibles.

Candle rolling

You will need: beeswax sheets in different colours and candle wicks (both available through the internet); metal ruler; pizza cutter.

Make it

Use the metal ruler and pizza cutter to cut triangular sheets of beeswax in two contrasting colours. (The triangles should be right-angled.) Cut a strip about 2cm wide off the diagonal side of one triangle. Lay the triangles one on top of the other so that the right angles line up, with the smaller sheet underneath.

Cut a piece of wick about 3cm longer than the diagonal of the triangle and lay it along the diagonal, close to the edge. Gently push the wick into the wax and carefully begin to roll up the candle from the diagonal edge. You should end up with a stripy, tapered candle.

Chat about it

Discuss the symbolism of candles and remember that Jesus said he was the light of the world. This means not just physical light, but the light in which we can try to understand and make sense of life.

Decorating wooden crosses

You will need: small wooden crosses (available on the internet); acrylic paint; small brushes.

Make it

Give each child a wooden cross and invite them to decorate it carefully, in whatever way they choose, with the acrylic paints.

Chat about it

Talk about why we associate the cross with Jesus and why it is such an important symbol to Christians. It is more than a membership badge. It is recognised worldwide. Why is it important to us? What does it mean? Suggest that the children might like to try holding their cross as they pray, or to put it somewhere at home where they will notice it, so that it can remind them of Jesus.

Cooking and/or eating

If you are using this session as the conclusion to a series, now might be an appropriate time to share food together.

If you wish, the children could try making bread (see the recipe in Appendix 2), or, if you have a bread machine, arrange for it to be making bread during the session, so that it is ready at a suitable time. Alternatively you could just bring a loaf of fresh bread. Make sure there is a table laid with a clean cloth, plates and a candle, with a jug of juice and cups. Invite the children to sit round the table together. Light a candle, say a grace, break the bread and share it.

Talk about how Jesus did this with his followers. What did it mean? Why did Jesus say he was the bread of life? Why is sharing bread still such a powerful symbol for us?

Discussion activities

Design a superhero

You will need: a large piece of paper or a flipchart on a stand; marker pens.

Talk to the children about what a hero is. They could tell you who their favourite comic book/TV heroes are. Then tell them that you'd like their help in designing a superhero. Use a large piece of paper or a flipchart and ask them to describe a superhero. Either invite the children to draw a piece of the superhero, or draw it yourself to their instruction.

Is it a male or female hero? Young or old? What does the face look like? Any hat or headwear? What sort of clothing? What kind of superpower? Any special equipment? The children will really enjoy this exercise as their ideas become ever more fantastic.

Against this background, ask the children what sort of a hero Jesus was. Could people tell he was a hero from his clothing or equipment? How is he different? How is he similar?

Favourite stories

Talk with the children about the stories they know about Jesus. Talk to them about which one is their favourite and why they like it. If someone knows a story that the other children don't know, they could tell it. Don't forget to share with them what your favourite story is and why.

What do these stories tell us about the sort of person, the sort of hero, Jesus was? What do our favourite stories about Jesus say about us?

Prayers

Cross prayers

Teach the children how to make the sign of the cross. Explain that it is a wordless prayer on its own, or can be used to start or finish prayers.

The Lord's Prayer

This is the prayer that Jesus taught us, so, if the children don't know it, teach it to them. If they are already familiar with it, work out a new way of praying it: you might try to find actions to fit the words so that the prayer can be prayed with the whole body, or create prayer stations around the church or other space for each line of the prayer.

Guided visualisation: Jesus washes the disciples' feet

Explore the story of Jesus washing his disciples' feet, using this guided visualisation. Read the text softly, allowing plenty of pauses for the children's imaginations to work.

Try to sit comfortably: back straight, shoulders relaxed, feet on the floor. Close your eyes and think about the wonderful planet we live on, with the great variety of habitat and life—oceans, deserts, mountains, forests, wastelands and farmlands. Think of our place in the world, in Europe, the islands of Great Britain, this country, our town. Think of the communities that make up our town—the shops, the organisations, our own church. Think of the building where we are now. Think of where you are in relation to the walls. Think how high the ceiling is above you. Feel the hardness of the floor beneath you.

I want to transport you to another place and another time—a hot, dusty country, nearly 2000 years ago. The walls around you could be wood or clay; there is a ceiling over your head. The floor is just as hard. The light comes from flickering oil lamps that cast unreal jumping shadows over the uneven walls. The sounds around you are the sounds of conversation. Outside, you might hear dogs barking or the footsteps of people passing, but otherwise silence. The stars in the sky are bright.

Jesus is there. You have hoped for a lot from Jesus. He could be destined to be king. You hoped he might fight and win for your country. You know he is a great man. You have seen him heal the sick, make the lame walk, and make the blind see. You know he has been sent by God. He is God's chosen one.

He kneels in front of you and looks at you. The eyes you know so well gaze at you. He knows you better than anyone else could ever know you. He knows all the good things you have done. He knows about all the times you haven't done as you should. He knows how worthy and how unworthy you are.

Your feet are hot and dusty and tired. He takes them in his cool, clean hands. He draws a bowl of water towards himself and washes your feet. You feel the warm, refreshing water flowing over your feet. Think how cleansing the water feels, and how gentle his hands are over your feet.

He looks at you again and you hear his words. You understand the significance. Jesus is acting as a servant to remind you that you should serve others. You understand that God turns things upside down. You understand that to follow the master is to become a servant. Spend some time thinking about the moment.

Now you need to come back to our room in our time. Feel the hardness of the floor; remember the position of the walls and ceiling of the room. Instead of the silence of the first century AD, you can hear sounds of our busy 21st-century life and you need to take your place within it again.

When you are ready, have a good stretch and open your eyes.

Stories of New Testament women

Key Bible focus

Then the angel told Mary, 'Don't be afraid! God is pleased with you, and you will have a son. His name will be Jesus. He will be great and will be called the Son of God Most High. The Lord God will make him king, as his ancestor David was. He will rule the people of Israel for ever, and his kingdom will never end.' ... Mary said, 'I am the Lord's servant! Let it happen as you have said.' And the angel left her.

LUKE 1:30–33, 38

Many of the New Testament women are surprisingly dynamic, given that women of their time were secondary to and dependent upon their husbands or sons. Consider, too, that histories from this time, including the Gospels, were written by men. We often lack detail about the women who were involved in the stories.

Although Mary's agreement to be the mother of Jesus may not seem particularly radical, at that time it certainly was. It was Mary who prompted Jesus to perform his first miracle at the wedding in Cana, and, even though most of Jesus' male friends had run away, she was present at the crucifixion.

Another Mary, Mary Magdalene, risked and incurred disdain when she anointed Jesus' feet, and she was ridiculed when she was the first to announce the resurrection.

• Many New Testament women were there, sometimes in the background, telling others about Jesus and showing in their daily lives that they were living for him as believers. How should we be witnessing for Jesus?

There are a number of stories of New Testament women that you might use for the story basis of your session.

- Mary the mother of Jesus: The story of the annunciation (Luke 1:26–38) or Jesus lost at the temple (Luke 2:41–51) or Jesus at the wedding feast at Cana (John 2:1–11) would be useful. You could also consider what Mary might have done or felt at other events in Jesus' life.
- Mary and Martha: Jesus' friends who chose different styles of following him. Use the story in Luke 10:38–42.
- Mary Magdalene: The story of the woman (often assumed to have been Mary Magdalene) anointing Jesus' feet (Luke 7:36–50) and of Mary Magdalene meeting Jesus after his resurrection (John 20:1–18).
- The Samaritan woman at the well: See John 4:7–42.

Displays for the church

Puppet show

If you are making Mary and Martha puppets (see p. 149), you might consider preparing a puppet show of the story to perform for the congregation. Perhaps a couple of children could write the script and others could make some props. You could even consider making a puppet theatre (or using a ready-made one).

Paint a crowd

You will need: paint in trays; felt-tip pens; face-shaped print blocks (you could use circular sponges and use felt-tip to add features later, or cut potatoes to make print blocks); brushes or sponges to apply paint; a good length of paper (size depending on number of children present); white card; felt or fabric to make a collage candle; glittery materials to make a flame; glue.

Make it

You could either have a candle already collaged on to your paper or allow the children to make it themselves. However, once the candle is in place at the centre of the paper, encourage the children to think about all the people they know or meet in their daily lives (family, friends, teachers, and so on). Show them how to use the print blocks to make face prints and invite them to print the faces of all the people they know around the candle. When the paint is dry, names could be added if you wish.

You might add a suitable caption to your crowd scene, such as 'Make your light shine, so that others will see the good that you do and will praise your Father in heaven' (Matthew 5:16).

Chat about it

Talk about how God is made known to others through the Bible that bears witness to him, but also through the daily lives of Christians everywhere. What do our lives tell the people we know about God? Would we want others to form an opinion of Christianity based on our behaviour?

Craft activities

Pots of perfume

Although there is nothing in any of the Gospel accounts to identify Mary Magdalene as the woman who anointed Jesus' feet with perfume and wiped them with her hair, she is associated with this story and is therefore often shown in stained-glass windows with long hair and holding an elaborate perfume jar. Whoever the woman really was, it's a good story.

This activity goes well with the perfume-making activity that follows. However, if you prefer, the pots can be made on their own. If so, you might wish to use larger containers.

Make it

Provide each child with a glass jar and invite them to use the glass
paints to decorate their jar. You may need to demonstrate how to
use the outlining paint and the colour.

Chat about it

Perfume bottles today are often made to look very special and
expensive. Why might this be?

Solid perfume

This recipe makes a type of solid perfume that has the benefit of
containing no alcohol. However, before undertaking this activity,
bear in mind that you need to check whether any of the children in
your group have a nut allergy, as a reaction could be triggered by the
almond oil. It may be possible to find a substitute oil, such as olive,
grapeseed or jojoba oil. Be aware that all oils deteriorate over time,
and olive oil may go 'off' more quickly than the other alternatives.

As the mixture is heated until it melts, care needs to be taken to
ensure that no one touches the hot liquid. It is important that only
short bursts in the microwave are used, to prevent overheating,
as beeswax in particular is flammable. Close adult supervision is
essential.

Make it

The quantity you make will depend on the number of children, but the ratio of ingredients is:

- Half a tablespoon petroleum jelly
- Half a tablespoon beeswax
- One tablespoon almond oil
- Twelve drops of essential oil

This quantity will make enough for about two small pots. You may want to make several small quantities to give everyone a turn at helping and perhaps to use different essential oils in each batch. The addition of beeswax makes a less oily finished product, and it can often be obtained from bee keepers, but, if you can't get hold of any, just double the quantity of petroleum jelly.

Put your measuring spoon in a mug of hot water. This will keep it warm and stop the wax from solidifying as soon as it touches the spoon. If you are using beeswax, you will need to melt it in a container in the microwave so that you can measure it out. Do this in short bursts of about 20 seconds, checking after each burst. Have the small pots ready and open.

When the wax is melted, dry the spoon with kitchen paper and use it to measure out half a tablespoon of wax into another container. Add the petroleum jelly and the almond oil. Return to the microwave for a further series of 20-second blasts, and stir after each blast with a cocktail stick. When the ingredients are melted together, add the essential oil, stir again with the cocktail stick and pour carefully into the containers. Leave to solidify before closing the lid to prevent condensation.

Chat about it

Why might Mary Magdalene have wanted to anoint Jesus' feet with perfume and wipe them with her hair? Talk also about the reaction of some of the disciples. Today perfumes are still often very costly. Why do you think they are so highly valued?

Hyacinths in pots

Hyacinths are often associated with Mary the mother of Jesus, so this activity will provide some leisure to think and talk about her. This activity is season-dependent and is best done in the autumn.

> You will need: terracotta flowerpots; acrylic paint; brushes; compost; hyacinth bulbs. Latex gloves may also be needed, since hyacinth bulbs can cause a reaction on some people's skin.

Make it

Provide each child with a flowerpot and invite them to decorate it. They might want to paint pictures of Mary or use the colours blue and white, which are usually associated with her. When the pots are finished, leave them to dry.

When the flowerpots are dry, show the children how to plant a hyacinth bulb. Invite each child to fill their freshly decorated pot with compost and a bulb.

Chat about it

Talk about the stories the children know about Mary. You might talk about why she said 'yes' to the angel Gabriel, or about how she felt when Jesus got lost at the temple. She was present when Jesus performed his first miracle, turning water into wine at the wedding in Cana, and she saw her son crucified a few years later. She knew from the beginning that he was very special, so how might this have made her feel at his birth and death?

Mary and Martha puppets

> You will need: a pair of socks for each child; glue; fabric and felt scraps; wool.

Make it

Show the children how (by tucking the toe in and back towards the heel to create a mouth) a sock can be used to make a puppet. You could show the children a finished puppet to help them understand how it will work. Invite the children to use the fabric and felt scraps and wool to glue on the features for their puppets—hair, eyes and so on. Allow them to dry. If each child makes two puppets, they can use them to act out the Mary and Martha rivalry.

Chat about it

Discuss the ways in which Mary and Martha were similar to and different from each other. Why might Martha have been so concerned with the housework when Jesus visited? How do we decide what is the most important thing for us to do?

Oil lamps

In Jesus' time, women looked after the oil lamps (remember the story of the wise and foolish girls waiting for the bridegroom?) so have a go at making models of oil lamps.

> You will need: air-hardening modelling clay; a selection of tools for shaping the clay; pictures of first-century oil lamps (found in books or on the internet).

Make it

Show the children some pictures of first-century oil lamps. Explain how they worked, with the central hole for filling the oil and the spout to house the wick. Invite the children to make their own models of oil lamps. It will be tricky to make them closed in, as some pictures show them, but a boat-shaped design, with a handle at one end and a spout at the other, should be possible. Make sure the children know that these are not working models and they shouldn't try to fill or light them.

Chat about it

Why was it important to look after oil lamps? What would it have been like to have them as your only source of light? You might want to light a candle to demonstrate the type of light they would have given. Jesus talked about how important it is not to hide one's light. What might he have meant? How did the New Testament women share their light?

Cooking

Entertaining cakes

Preparing food and drink was the preserve of women in New Testament times. When Jesus visited Mary and Martha, Martha prepared the food (and expected Mary to help her), and, when he was in Samaria, Jesus asked the woman at the well for a drink.

> You will need: plain fairy cakes, either bought or home-made; icing sugar; water or lemon juice; sugar sprinkles and/or small sweets, such as chocolate buttons or dolly mixtures; mixing bowl; spoons; food colouring (optional); small bowls (optional).

Make it

Make a simple glacé icing by mixing icing sugar with a little water or lemon juice. Make sure it isn't too runny: it needs to stay on the cakes. If you want to make a few bowls of different coloured icing, divide the mixture between the bowls and add a little food colouring to each one. Invite the children to decorate the fairy cakes in whatever way they please. You could leave the icing to harden and allow the children to take their cakes home or eat them when it's time for a break.

Chat about it

Talk about whether the children enjoyed the activity and why. What would it be like to have to make all the food all the time? Is there someone in your house who always does the cooking? Is it important to try not to be busy all the time? Why? Do we always notice when someone is being too busy at helping us? Martha seems to have been working hard to make sure Jesus had the best food to eat. Why do we take trouble when a guest comes to our house for a meal?

Games

Photo-fit

Mary Magdalene had some difficulty in persuading the other disciples to understand and believe that she had seen the risen Jesus, so try this game, involving some difficult explanations. (It may be too challenging for younger children.)

Prepare some cards, each with a simple line-drawn picture of a common item, such as a car, house, fork or rabbit. Issue each child with a piece of paper and a pencil.

As the children take it in turns to choose a card, they describe how to draw the item but without saying what it is. They need to use mathematic or geometric instructions, such as 'Draw a square in the bottom half of the page; then, on top, draw a triangle so that one side is the top of the square and the other two sides are equal; the height of the triangle should be half the height of the square.'

The children in the audience should draw what is described. See who gets closest to the original picture.

Discussion activities

Refraction

> You will need: prisms or glass shapes used in rainbow makers; a light source (the sun on a fine day, or a bright and focused torch).

Show the children how the white light from the sun or a torch, when it shines through a glass prism or a crystal, can be split into different colours to make a rainbow. You could recall Noah's rainbow and its significance, if you wished.

Talk about how Jesus told us that he was the light of the world. We sometimes think of Christians as trying to live lives that shine like lights, but we should remember that it is not we who are shining. We are just reflecting, refracting and diffusing God's light. God's light is bright and pure and clear. What shines through us is sometimes distorted and impure, but we should still allow it to shine as well as we can.

The women in the New Testament were not afraid to let their allegiance to God and Jesus be seen. They were willing to allow his light to shine through them.

Prayers

Candle prayers

The New Testament women we have been learning about witnessed for Jesus by telling others about him and by living their lives as he had shown them. As each child lights a candle, pray that God will help us to bear witness to his light in our lives, too. Perhaps each candle could be taken to illuminate a different part of your room or church. This would be most effective in a poorly lit room, but don't take risks that children will trip while holding lighted candles.

Guided visualisation: Mary Magdalene at the resurrection

Try to sit comfortably—back straight, shoulders relaxed, feet on the floor. Close your eyes and remember the colour of the sky outside on a bright, clear, sunlit day. Think of the sun travelling across the sky, turning it through all the different shades of blue. The lightest translucent powder blue slowly fades towards a luminous swimming-pool blue. Perhaps, as the earth turns, wispy clouds begin to gather, becoming tinged with pink; then the sky sinks to a glowing indigo as the first stars come out, and then deepest, thickest midnight blue, studded with stars. Imagine the clouds rolling across the sky as everything darkens before dawn.

I want to take you back to one morning in another country and another century, nearly 2000 years ago. It is very early in the morning and very cold. The dawn light is crawling into the sky, giving everything a steel-grey tinge. The ground is wet with dew. It soaks your feet as you walk through the grass. You can hear creatures around you beginning to stir and rustle after the long, dark night. Your limbs feel heavy and still full of sleep.

You have a sad duty to perform. You remember the cruel, tortured death of Jesus, in whom all your hope was centred. It's as if your hope and life have died with him. Now you are coming back to Jesus' body, to finish preparing it for the tomb. You shiver as you think of the cold, dark, dry place where his body has rested.

As you enter the garden where he is, the sky continues to brighten with a pinkish tinge. It paints the tops of the trees with a rosy light and casts long, thin shadows on the ground. Birds begin to sing their first few notes and a gentle breeze stirs the branches. You can smell fresh vegetation—the garden around you growing and waking to a new day—but you cannot join it because, for you, there are only the depths of sorrow.

As you turn a corner, you see a figure. You don't expect to see anyone, but someone is there. The sunlight bursts through with a bright, golden, glorious light, so bright that you can barely see. It is as if all of nature, the force of all life in the universe, is concentrated on this small space. Your senses are overwhelmed and flooded with joy, and your heart leaps. What you see can hardly be true. Almost in slow motion, the figure turns to you... reaches out a hand... and calls you by name. You know it is him. You feel suspended in the moment. This is a turning point in your life, everything before leading up to it, and everything from now leading away from it. Feel what it is like to be in that moment.

Now we need to return to our room. Allow the bright, golden light to fade gently and slowly, as it does when the sun rises in the sky. The sky takes on the look of polished bronze, fading to pink, and then the delicate translucent powder blue of a clear, bright day.

When you're ready, open your eyes and have a stretch.

Guided visualisation: Jesus meets the Samaritan woman at the well

Make sure you are sitting comfortably, with your back straight and your shoulders relaxed. Close your eyes and think about where we live—our beautiful, green, abundant part of the world. It's like that because we have plenty of water. It falls from the skies, gently or in torrents, and it flows in streams and rivers. Our island is surrounded by the sea.

I want to take you to another time and place where the air is dry and the ground is dusty; rainfall is uncertain. There are plants thriving but less lush greenery. Water is precious: it is valued and never wasted. The source of clean fresh water is the well in your village. It is a meeting place, too, as people need to visit it every day. Friends are made, news exchanged and help offered at the side of the well.

One day, you are late getting to the well. Everyone has collected their water for the day and gone home again. The day is hot and dry, and the walk in the blazing sun is unpleasant. You notice that someone is sitting by the well—a stranger. As you approach, you notice what he looks like. You know somehow that he is someone you can trust. He raises his head to look at you, and you feel you have known him all your life. There is such gentleness and kindness in his eyes that you know he is a friend. You stop to speak to him. What might you say? How do you feel, talking to him?

He asks you to let him have some water and you gladly fill a cup from the bucket of water you have just drawn from the well. Feel the cool, clean freshness of the water as you dip the cup into it. Watch how the waterdrops sparkle in the sunlight as they fall back into the bucket. Remember how precious this water is. Watch him as he accepts the water and drinks it.

He returns the cup and thanks you. What does he say? How does he look? How do you feel to be thanked for such an insignificant service?

You ask who he is and he begins to tell you, but you don't quite understand what he means. He says he can give you the water of life. It will never run out, and people who drink it will never be thirsty. Think how much more sustaining and valuable this water of life must be—how much cleaner and brighter and cooler than the water from your well. Think how it would feel to have a source of water that could never fail. You would no longer need to make the tedious journey to the well, but you could always wash and be clean and drink and be sustained.

You understand how important this moment is. You have understood something here about who the stranger is and about who you are. You want to fix the memory in your mind, so try to see the whole picture—the dusty village with its well, the haze of heat rising from the ground, vague outlines of distant hills, the little houses where others shelter from the heat, a few chickens scratching in the dust, the feel of sand and dirt on your feet.

Fix the stranger in your memory—his gentle, searching gaze, his strength, his strange words, the way he seemed to know you. Remember the water you drew from the well, how cool and fresh it was; remember the sparkle of the droplets in the sun; remember the sound it made as it was poured.

Remember how you imagined what the water of life might be like, which the stranger said he could give you. What did he mean? How will it affect you? Now you have fixed this memory in your mind, you can take it away with you and think about it whenever you want to.

Now we need to return to our room, so take another look around at the dusty, dry landscape beyond the village. Think about the smell of hot, parched soil and imagine you can begin to feel a moisture in the air. Notice as the dryness begins to admit the fragrance of growing grass and moist soil that has been blessed by rain. Remember the abundance of water we have here, in streams, rivers and lakes.

When you're ready, open your eyes and have a stretch.

— Theme 15 —

Stories of early church heroes

Key Bible focus

When Saul had almost reached Damascus, a bright light from heaven suddenly flashed around him. He fell to the ground and heard a voice that said, 'Saul! Saul! Why are you so cruel to me?' 'Who are you?' Saul asked. 'I am Jesus,' the Lord answered. 'I am the one you are so cruel to. Now get up and go into the city, where you will be told what to do.'

ACTS 9:3–6

The heroes of the early church were an energetic bunch and there are plenty of stories to choose from in the Acts of the Apostles. The stories are full of miracles and escapes from prison. There is also a lot of soul-searching, as it gradually became clear (and perhaps went against the grain, for some) that the church needed to include Gentiles as well as the nation of Israel.

There are many ways to tell these stories. Drama or hot-seating could help the children enter into and understand the stories better. Suggested Bible verses are listed below, but there is no need to be limited by this list. For example, if your patronal saint is one of the founders of the early church, you might want to explore him instead.

- Philip and the Ethiopian official (Acts 8:26–39)
- The conversion of Paul (Acts 9:1–19)
- Peter's vision (Acts 10:9–16, 34–48)
- Peter escapes from prison (Acts 12:6–19)
- Barnabas journeys with Paul (Acts 13 and 14)
- Paul and Silas in prison (Acts 16:16–40)

- These heroes of the early church worked hard but they let Jesus take control of where they should go and what they should do, even when it was unexpected. How should we hand control of our lives to Jesus?

Displays for the church

Christian world

> You will need: a laptop and internet access; a prepared map of the world (see Appendix 3) drawn on to a large sheet of paper; fish-shaped print blocks; smiley face print blocks; paint in ten shades of red or green and one shade of light blue; trays; sponges; hand-washing equipment.

Make it

Show the children the BBC Civilisations website so that they can see for themselves how Christianity has grown and spread around the world: www.bbc.co.uk/religion/tools/civilisations/.

If you don't have computer facilities in your room, you will need to have looked at the website in advance and noted down the details of the spread of Christianity over the centuries. You could pencil these on to the map so that the children can follow the spread and complete the map.

Then invite the children to fill in the map using printing techniques. Use the light blue paint and the fish print blocks to fill in the seas. Then use shades of either red or green to print smiley faces or fingerprint the land. Use the darkest shade of red or green to print over the countries that became Christian in the first 200 years after Christ, use the next darkest colour for AD200 to 400, and so on, eventually using the lightest shade for 1800–2000.

Alternatively you could prepare the map as a permanent hanging, using fabric.

Chat about it

Talk about how the spread of Christianity started with the struggles of the few earliest Christians, a long time ago and a long way away. Talk about what enabled the faith to grow so spectacularly.

St Paul's light show

Tell the story of Paul's conversion on the road to Damascus. Discuss how you might present it dramatically and work with the children to put their ideas into practice. You could use an OHP projector and screen and move card silhouette figures around to tell the story, or perhaps you could rig up a sheet with a strong light behind it so that the children can use their own silhouettes to perform the story for the rest of the congregation.

Children's church noticeboard

> You will need: a cork pinboard (obtainable from DIY shops); card to cut up for decoration; glue; other media, such as paint or pens to decorate.

Make it

If you don't have a noticeboard for children in your church, this might be a good opportunity to make one.

Discuss with the children how your board might be decorated. If your group has a name, you might prepare some cut-out letters to form the name, which the children could decorate with pens or paint before gluing them on the board. You could do the same with any emblem you may have. Talk also about any other symbols that the children think are appropriate, such as a cross, flame, water drop or dove shape. Arrange the customised decorations and glue them to the board.

You might want to consider preparing particular areas of the board for certain types of notice—for example, an area where the details of your next meeting will be displayed or one where children might leave prayer requests. (Ensure that there is a pencil and supply of paper nearby for such requests.)

When the board is finished, find somewhere prominent to fix it where everyone will see it.

If you are concerned about using pins, the idea would also work for a magnetic board. Alternatively, attach a lattice of tape or matt ribbon so that it criss-crosses the board, so that (small) notices can be slid behind it.

Chat about it

Talk about how important communication is. It was vital for the early Christians to stay in touch and help each other in their faith, and it is vital for us too. Perhaps your noticeboard will help you to keep in touch.

Miniature church

This project could take some time, so you might prefer to do a really good job by spreading it over a number of sessions.

> You will need: a large cardboard box (prepared with emulsion paint if you wish); card; modelling clay and/or other modelling materials; paint; pens; scissors, glue.

Make it

Early Christians often met in houses but, when there were too many people to do this, people began to build churches to meet in. Explain that the children now have an opportunity to design and build their own church.

There are a number of ways in which you might tackle this project, so you need to decide how you will approach it. If you use an old building, you might research how it might have looked when it was first built and make a model of it, or you could make a model of your church as it is now, or you could ask the children to imagine an ideal church and create a model of how they would like it to be.

Invite the children to work together to create the model. The walls can be painted outside and inside, with doors and windows cut into them. (You will probably need to do this yourself with a modelling knife, away from small fingers.) The children could make the furnishings (pews, chairs, altar, pulpit and font), using whatever modelling materials you have provided. Don't forget to make people to go inside. If you wish, you could add labels.

Chat about it

Talk about how we use our church and how it is part of our lives. Discuss how it might have been part of other people's lives in the past. If you're making an 'ideal' church, in what ways is it different from your own church? How is it better?

Don't forget to talk about how you can have a church without a building. The church is the people. Just as Peter discovered, we should welcome anybody who wishes to come.

Craft activities

Fishing game

You will need: a deep cardboard box; short garden canes; thread; small magnets that can be tied on; clean plastic milk containers cut into fish shapes (this can be done with scissors or a craft knife); acrylic paint; metal paperclips.

Make it

First of all, prepare the 'tank'. Decorate the inside of the cardboard box by painting it with suitably watery colours. Leave it to dry.

Give each child a few plastic fish shapes and invite them to paint the fish in bright colours. When the paint is dry, they could use a pen to mark scales and eyes. Slip a paperclip on to the nose of each fish. If you wish to secure it, make a small hole in the nose of the fish and slide one end of the clip through the hole.

Next, issue each child with a short cane, a length of thread or fine cord and a magnet. Tie the magnet to the thread and the thread to the cane to make a fishing rod. The magnets should pick up the paper-clipped fish.

Chat about it

Jesus told his disciples to go out and fish for people, and they continued to do this after his death and resurrection. They allowed God to guide them to the people they needed to talk to—those who were ready to listen.

Fish badges

You will need: clean plastic milk containers cut into fish shapes (this can be done with scissors or a craft knife); acrylic paint; safety pins; good-quality sticky tape, such as insulation tape; pens.

Make it

Cut a fish-shaped master stencil and use it to mark as many fish shapes as you need on to the plastic cut from old milk containers. Each badge shape will need to be painted with two coats of acrylic paint. This can either be done by the children (although drying time will be needed) or prepared in advance. Use a selection of colours, so that the children have a choice.

To make the badges, give each child a fish shape and ask them to write their name on the shape (painted side) and then decorate it like a fish. Using glittery gel pens gives a scaly effect. When this is done, a small safety pin can be secured to the back with insulation tape.

Before doing this activity, check that the pen the children will use to write their names will work on the paint. You may need to buy a fine-nibbed permanent black felt pen.

Chat about it

Early Christians lived in fear of being arrested, imprisoned or even put to death for their beliefs. They often used the fish as a sign that they were Christian, so that other Christians would be able to recognise them without having to openly declare themselves. It was like the sign for a secret society.

Saintly chain

You will need: long, narrow strips of paper; scissors; pencil; felt-tip pens or paint; pencils.

Make it

Show the children how to fold their strip of paper concertina-fashion so that the folds are on top of each other to each side. Draw a fish shape or, if you prefer, a person shape, but make sure that the nose and tail (or hands and feet) touch the folded edges. Show the children how to cut round the shape, leaving enough area at the edges uncut. Unfold the chain to reveal a line of fishes (or people).

Invite the children to have a go. If you wish, they could fill in detail and colour their line of figures.

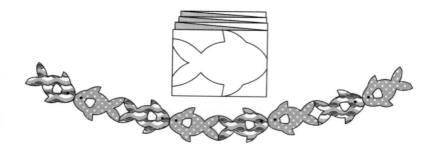

Chat about it

Talk about how we have depended for our faith on a succession of people, all telling each other about Jesus, going right back to his earliest followers. One break in the chain and it all falls apart.

Prison break pictures

> You will need: white A4 paper or thin card; paint; brushes; pens; dark brown A4 card; glue; scissors.

Make it

Give each child a piece of paper and invite them to paint a picture of 'freedom': how freedom would feel, what it might look like, or a place where the children might feel free. They should leave a margin of about 2.5cm round the edges.

While the pictures are drying, show the children how to cut a set of double doors in the brown card, leaving a frame of about 2.5cm all round the edges. The children could use the pens to draw nail heads and heavy handles and hinges to make the doors look like heavy-duty prison doors.

When the pictures are dry, mount them behind the prison doors so that, when the doors open, freedom is on the other side. If you wish, you could use collage to place an angel on the inside of the prison door.

Chat about it

How might it have felt to be locked up in prison and in fear for your life? How might people like Peter, Paul or Silas have felt to have an angel release them?

Games

Fishing game

If you have made a fishing game, you might take some time to play it together. Talk about how much harder it is to catch real fish that can swim away. How hard do you think Jesus' first followers found it to persuade other people, who had never met Jesus, to believe in him?

Feely games

When Paul first encountered Jesus, he was struck blind. People who can't see rely more heavily on their other senses.

You will need: feely boxes or opaque cloth bags; a selection of objects to put inside; paper and pencils. Choose household objects with a variety of different textures (for example, cabbage leaf, water-filled balloon, spoon, pencil, pan scourer, and so on), but make sure you don't use anything sharp or splintery.

Play it

Let children take turns to feel the objects without being able to see them. If they think they can identify an object, they need to write it down. Check what the children thought they were feeling, then empty the boxes or bags to see what was inside.

Chat about it

Even though Paul was blinded when Jesus was first revealed to him, his blindness enabled him to see who Jesus was. After that, perhaps Paul trusted more in God's vision than his own. How would we manage without sight?

Discussion activities

Ichthus

This activity fits in well with the fish-related craft activities. Show the children the Christian fish symbol and ask if they have seen it before. Talk about how early Christians were persecuted and often suffered greatly for their faith, and how they used the symbol of the fish as a secret sign, so that they could identify other Christians. Cut out some pieces of card and use them to write the words (in Greek, with a translation on the back):

- Iesus Christos Theou Uios Soter
- Jesus Christ, Son of God, Saviour

Slide the cards one over the other to make the Greek word 'Ichthus'. There may be a child in your group who is a dinosaur fan and knows about ichthyosaurs (which translates as 'fish lizard').

Epistles

Paul wrote a lot of letters to Christians in early churches to give them guidance and to nurture them in their new faith. You might like to have a look at a few passages from his letters in the Bible.

Talk to the children about how Paul might have kept in touch today. They might want to write their own messages (perhaps to go on your noticeboard), or they might wish to send emails to your church's leaders.

Prayers

Prayer journey

Several chapters of the Acts of the Apostles describe the journeys that the apostles took to tell everyone about Jesus. Try a walking prayer. If it is a fine day, you could lead the children round the outside of your church. If it is wet or very noisy outdoors, stay inside. Walk slowly and thoughtfully round the church, stopping at different points with a prayer or reflection. For instance, at the porch you might pray for those who enter the building; under a window you could pray for the light of Christ to shine on his people; the bell tower might prompt a prayer for Jesus' message to be heard beyond the church walls, and the churchyard could be a place to pray for those who have gone before us.

Guided visualisation in a church

The heroes of the early church founded what we know as the church today. Of course, the church is really the people who are part of the body of Christ, but often the buildings where we meet are special and have a special atmosphere. This guided visualisation celebrates the continuous centuries of worship in one place. You will probably need to adapt it for your circumstances. Read the text slowly and softly, allowing plenty of pauses for the children's imaginations to work.

Make sure you are sitting comfortably, with your back straight and your shoulders relaxed. Close your eyes. Now try to visualise the world and its place among the stars, our country and its place in the world, our town, the surroundings of our church and ourselves within it.

Think about how long this place has been here and what this area might have looked like before the town/village was built. Imagine what it might have been like to watch this great building rise slowly skywards at the time when it was built. Consider the time, skill and energy that have gone into the making of the church. The people are long gone but their dedication is remembered here in the stones, wood and glass around us. What would it have been like to be part of this construction process?

Consider all the people who have visited this church through all the years. Think about how many thousands, maybe millions, have walked through these doors—rich, poor, clever, active, disabled, troubled, happy, distressed, unsure.

What have they been seeking? Shelter, safety, peace, forgiveness, grace, security, love, fellowship, community, comfort?

They have come at all times in our history, wearing rich brocades and silks or just the best clothes they could find or mend, simple clothing or ornate, sweeping gowns and hats or casual jeans and backpacks.

Imagine the different things they have seen within these walls—the decorations of flowers and ribbons for a wedding; the sombre starkness of Lent; the glittering of many lights at Christmas; joyous crowds at times of celebration; a single flickering candle at a lonely vigil.

Think about the different sounds—the joyful pealing of bells or the muffled tolling of a single bell; the choir praising God; the beauty of a single voice; tears, laughter and mumbled prayers; the breaking of bread; the sound of many people silent together or the silence of the empty building.

Imagine the different smells—the heady scent of summer flowers filling the building; heavy incense; rich Christmas evergreens; people crowded in.

Think about the different textures and surfaces—cool grainy stone; polished glass; burnished metals; warm, fragrant waxed wood; fabrics lovingly worked by unknown hands.

Think about the feelings the church has been a focus for—grief, joy, exuberance, fear, loss, peace, thankfulness and bliss.

Remember that we are now part of the life of this place. We are one of those thousands, maybe millions, of visitors. We can take away the memory and feeling of this place, which has been informed by so many people and experiences, and we can leave the shadow of our feelings and experiences here to enrich the life of our church.

Now we need to come back to our place and time here. So remember where we are, here in this church. Visualise how it sits in this town and how our town makes up part of our country, part of our planet.

When you are ready, you can open your eyes and have a stretch.

Can we be heroes for Jesus?

Key Bible focus

Be ready! Let the truth be like a belt around your waist, and let God's justice protect you like armour. Your desire to tell the good news about peace should be like shoes on your feet.
EPHESIANS 6:14–15

This session brings the story of Bible heroes right up to date by exploring how we can be heroes for Jesus.

There are no specific stories for this session. You could base it on biblical texts such as the parable of the talents (Matthew 25:14–30; Luke 19:11–27) or Paul's instructions to wear the full armour of God (Ephesians 6:10–18) or his encouragement to bear fruit in the wisdom and knowledge of the Spirit (Colossians 1:9–14). It could also be a chance to look at non-biblical figures who have followed Jesus. You might include stories about modern saints such as Mother Teresa of Calcutta or Gladys Aylward, or perhaps people who were or are local to you.

• There are still heroes around us today. As God gave his heroes of the Old and New Testaments particular gifts or talents to serve him, he does the same for us. What gifts has God given us and how can we best use them?

Displays for the church

A hero for Jesus today

> You will need: lining paper; marker pens; pencils and paper.

Make it

Talk with the children about what attributes a modern-day hero for God might have. You might refer to the Ephesians passage if you are using it. What might the modern armour of God consist of? How might Paul have described it if he had been writing today?

Some attributes might be more obvious: for instance, the children are probably likely to be able to come up with 'prayer' and 'showing kindness and compassion'. You could also discuss whether strength, for instance, might be necessary, and, if so, what sort of strength. How might a hero for Jesus differ from most people's idea of a hero? Make a list together of what would be required.

Together with the children, use this list to construct a recipe for today's hero for Jesus. For example, 'To an open and compassionate heart, add a generous measure of gentleness; stiffen the mixture with courage, season with experience and leaven with prayer.'

Draw round one of the children on a length of lining paper, using a marker pen, and invite them to write the recipe inside the outline. Be imaginative with the lettering and the way the lines of the recipe are positioned, so that arms, legs and torso are filled. The children could illustrate or decorate any space left.

Craft activities

Making mirrors

> You will need: small handbag mirrors or plastic mirrored A4 sheets, which can be cut to size; hardboard; emulsion paint; glue; items to decorate frames (for example, 'jewels', beads, shells, painted pasta).

Make it

Make sure the hardboard pieces are cut to size so that a mirror fits on each one with a margin of roughly 4cm all round. Paint the hardboard with white emulsion to give a good base and then glue the mirrors into place.

Give the children the mounted mirrors and allow them to decorate them by gluing false jewels or other decorative pieces to the hardboard margin round the mirror. This works particularly well if, later in the session, the children can use the mirrors they have made as an aid to a meditation on themselves.

Chat about it

What is it that makes me special? Why are we unique individuals?

Self-sculptures

You will need: air-drying clay; some modelling implements if desired; covers for your work surfaces.

Make it

Older children in particular might enjoy doing sculptures of themselves. A head-and-shoulders model is likely to be easier and less frustrating than a full-length depiction, since it will be difficult to ensure that arms and legs stay on and take the weight of the sculpture.

Chat about it

What is it that makes me special? Why are we unique individuals?

Decorating T-shirts

You will need: cheap white T-shirts in various suitable sizes; brushes; fabric paints; water to wash brushes and hands; plastic bags; cardboard; iron and ironing board, or a set of instructions to take home.

Make it

Help the children to choose a T-shirt of the right size. To prevent paint from seeping through from front to back, put a sheet of cardboard into a plastic bag and place it inside the T-shirt. Invite the children to decorate their T-shirt using the fabric paint. Encourage them to use the paint sparingly or it will take a very long time to dry.

Suggest that they illustrate Jesus or their favourite Bible hero, or perhaps Jesus on the front and an Old Testament Bible hero on the back, allowing time to dry between pictures.

Fabric paint usually needs to be fixed by ironing. If the paint is dry, this can be done before the children go home. If not, you will need to send instructions home with the children.

Chat about it

Who is your favourite Bible hero? What do you especially remember about the story? Why is he or she your favourite hero?

Cooking

Gingerbread people

> You will need: enough gingerbread or biscuit dough for the number of children in your group (see Appendix 2 for a recipe); baking parchment; baking trays; person-shaped cutters; rolling-pin.

Make it

You will need to prepare a quantity of gingerbread or biscuit dough, or, if time allows, let the children help to make it.

Provide the children with people-shaped cutters and some mini sugar-covered chocolate beans or raisins with which to decorate their people. Place each biscuit on a square of baking parchment, marked with the child's name, and then on a baking sheet. Bake them either on the premises or, if you have no kitchen facilities, at a friendly neighbour's house. If neither of these is possible, the children could take the biscuits home unbaked, with instructions on how to bake them at home.

As with any food activity, check whether any child has allergies. If the biscuit recipe you are using contains egg, make sure the children don't eat the raw dough. You will need hand-washing facilities for before and after this activity. If you have no water connection, a plastic washing-up bowl, water warmed in a kettle, some soap and towels are adequate.

Games

Quiz

Organise a quiz about the Bible heroes that you have looked at, including Jesus.

Who am I?

Prepare cards showing the names of some of the Bible heroes you have looked at. Give a card to each child. They should read the name and mentally 'get into character' but not show anyone else.

Invite the children to 'meet and greet' each other. They should talk to other children to see if they can find out who everyone else is. The only rules are that they can't ask 'Who are you?' and they cannot tell anyone else directly who their character is.

Prayers

Thanksgiving for heroes

To conclude the series of sessions, give thanks for all the Bible heroes you have learned about. You could include other heroes of faith: the children might be able to suggest some. Perhaps they could each supply a line of the prayer. Thank God for the example of all heroes of faith, and for all that we can learn about God from them. God's heroes do not have to be world leaders or be rich or powerful, so ask God to help us all to follow in their footsteps.

Meditation: Me

If the children have made mirror frames, this makes a good starting-point for a meditation on themselves. Encourage the children to look at different parts of their faces and think about what is special about them. They are all unique and they are all loved by God and are part of God's family.

Invite children to take a mirror. Read the meditation below slowly and softly, leaving pauses for the children to reflect and think.

Hold your mirror in your hands lightly but securely. Make sure you are sitting comfortably: check that your back is straight and your shoulders are relaxed. Close your eyes. Think about the room around us. Think about how it fits into the surrounding streets or lanes and how they fit into our town/village. Think about what the people near to our room might be doing. Be aware of this space enclosed by the walls, the height of the ceiling above you, and the hardness of the floor below you.

Now slowly and gently open your eyes and focus only on the mirror you hold in your hand. Without moving the mirror, look at what you can see of the room around you. Then focus on the centre of the mirror. Look at your own reflection. Study it. Don't move your face while you do this.

Take in the colour of your hair, its texture and style. Examine your skin, its flaws and perfections, its texture and colour.

Look at the shape of your face, and where your eyes, nose and mouth are positioned. Maybe you can trace a family likeness to other people in your family, maybe not.

Look at your mouth, its size and shape. Think about the things your mouth has said in the past, both good and bad. How are these things expressed in your face now? How have they left their mark? What is its usual expression—smiling or sad?

Look at your nose, its size and shape. Think about how it gives your face definition. Look closely at your eyelids, eyelashes and eyebrows. Then look at your eyes themselves. Look at the colour of the iris. Perhaps there's more than one colour, more than one light. Look at the depth of the pupil. How are the things your eyes have seen expressed in your face?

Remember that there is no one else in the world who is like you. You are unique, one of a kind. The people who love you do so not because you are especially good or clever, but because you are especially you. God loves you because you are especially you. You do not need to earn his love, you cannot deserve it, but he gives it freely because you are you.

As you look at your reflection, think about what you might be. How you might grow? What sort of person might you become?

What are your dreams? What do you hope for? What do you want to achieve? How do you want others to see you? What do you think might be the most valuable achievement you could strive for? It might not be achievement of work or qualification. It might be a quality you might want to develop or appreciate. See yourself for a moment as that future person.

Now we need to come back to this place and this time. Look at yourself again as you are today. Feel the life in your body and allow awareness of the room to come back to you—the hardness of the floor, the space of the room bounded by walls and ceiling. Come back into our room and understand its place in our community, our town/village.

When you are ready, have a stretch.

Sample session plan

Two-hour session plan for Abraham

Key Bible focus: Genesis 12:1–2

Time	Activity
0.00–0.10	Registration and welcome
0.10–0.15	Story: God's promises
0.15–0.30	Angel cakes
0.30–0.50	Trinity icon collage
0.50–1.00	Flicking stars into space
1.00–1.10	Break with angel cakes
1.10–1.25	Trinity spinners
1.25–1.35	Truth or lie game
1.35–1.50	Sand pictures
1.50–2.00	Sandy prayers

— Appendix 2 —

Recipes

Biscuit or gingerbread dough

You will need:

- 300g plain flour
- A pinch of salt
- 1 teaspoon baking powder
- 1 teaspoon nutmeg or ground ginger (if making ginger biscuits)
- 100g butter or margarine
- 100g soft brown sugar
- 2 eggs
- 60g golden syrup
- Mixing bowl
- Mixing spoon or hand-held mixer
- Baking parchment or greaseproof paper
- Flour
- Rolling-pins
- Biscuit cutters
- Pencils
- Hand-washing facilities

Put the flour, salt, baking powder and nutmeg into a bowl. Rub in the butter or margarine, then stir in the sugar. Beat the eggs with the golden syrup and add to the mixture. Mix well either by hand or with a hand-held mixer.

Divide the dough into pieces, enough for one per child. Have a surface ready for rolling: pieces of well-floured baking parchment or greaseproof paper on your normal table covering work well and are disposable later. The dough should be rolled to about 5mm thickness and then the biscuits can be cut out.

Ask the children to place their biscuits on a named piece of baking parchment. The biscuits will need to be baked in an oven pre-heated to Gas Mark 3 or 160°C for about 18 minutes, but keep an eye on them.

Modelling dough

You will need:

- 2 cups plain flour
- 1 cup salt
- 2 teaspoons cream of tartar
- 2 tablespoons cooking oil
- 2 cups boiling water
- Food dye if desired

Mix the flour, salt, cream of tartar and cooking oil together in a bowl. Pour in two cups of boiling water (just boiled, straight from the kettle). If you want the dough coloured, adding food dye to the water will help the even distribution of colour through the mix. Knead with a hand-held mixer or machine (it will be too hot for your hands). Allow the dough to cool (but don't let it crust over) before packing it away in a plastic bag.

Bread

You will need:

- 400g strong plain flour
- 2 level teaspoons sugar
- 2 level teaspoons fast-action dried yeast
- 1.5 level teaspoons salt
- 230ml plus 5 tablespoons warm water
- 2 tablespoons olive oil
- Two mixing bowls
- Mixing spoon
- Sieve
- Clean tea towel
- Greaseproof paper
- Baking tray
- Cooling rack

Sift the flour, sugar, yeast and salt into a bowl. Add the water and oil and knead well. Cover with a clean tea towel and leave in a warm place for approximately one hour until the dough has doubled in size.

Turn the dough out on to a floured surface and knead again until smooth. Divide the dough and shape as required. Place your finished shapes on a greased and floured baking tray. Cover with the tea towel and leave to rise in a warm place again until the shapes have doubled in size.

Bake in the centre of a pre-heated oven at 190°C/Gas Mark 5 for 45–50 minutes for a loaf or 15 minutes for rolls. They are cooked when they are golden brown and sound hollow when you tap their base. Cool on a wire rack.

Templates

Joseph: 3D star shapes

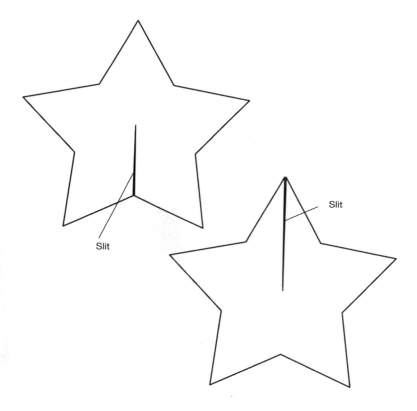

Slit

Slit

Ruth: Cat shapes for bird-scarer activity

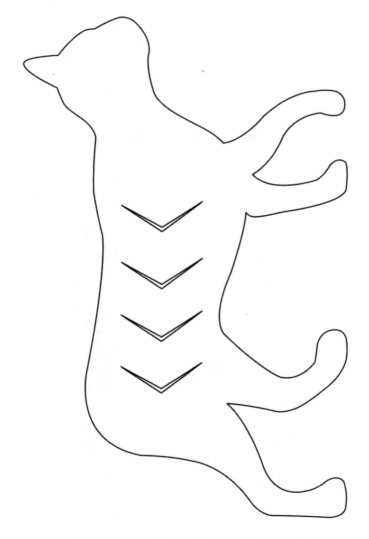

Reproduced with permission from *Not Sunday, Not School: Bible Heroes!* by Eleanor Zuercher, published by Barnabas for Children 2013 (www.barnabasinchurches.org.uk)

Solomon: Owl template

Elijah: Raven template

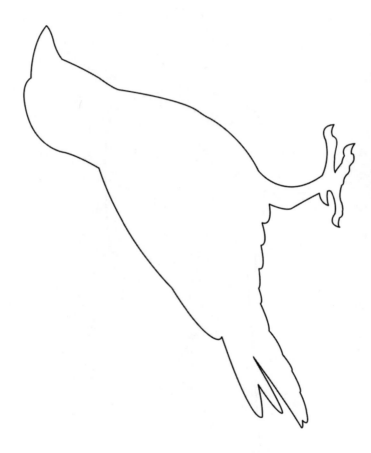

Reproduced with permission from *Not Sunday, Not School: Bible Heroes!* by Eleanor Zuercher, published by Barnabas for Children 2013 (www.barnabasinchurches.org.uk)

Old Testament prophets: Figures for the furnace

You will need four of these figures.

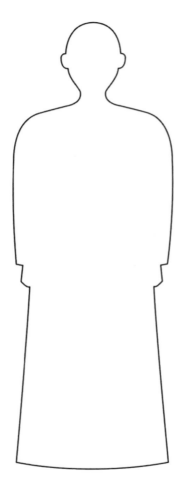

Old Testament prophets: Lion mask template

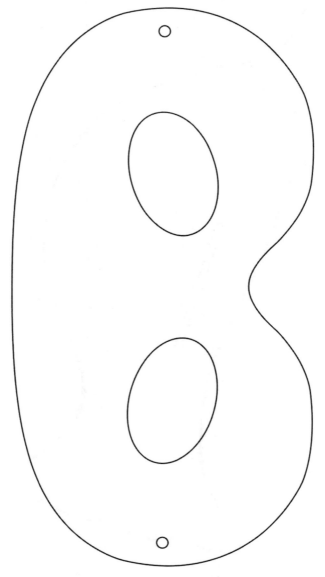

Reproduced with permission from *Not Sunday, Not School: Bible Heroes!* by Eleanor Zuercher, published by Barnabas for Children 2013 (www.barnabasinchurches.org.uk)

John the Baptist: Dove template

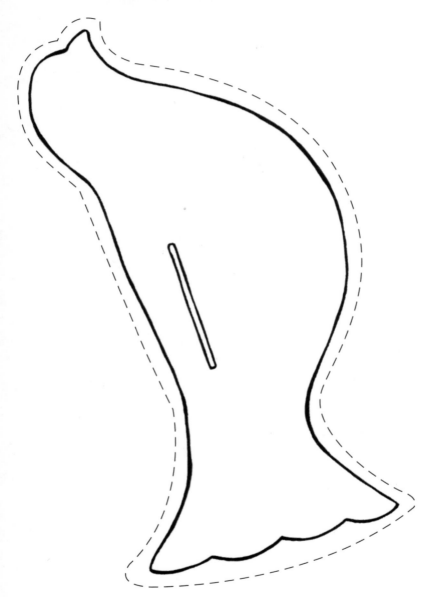

Early church heroes: Christian world

Bibliography

Listed below are the resources that inspired the ideas for this book and the original session on which it is based. A diverse selection of Bible translations is recommended when trying to find the right language for a particular story: the best won't always be the children's version.

Alongside Christian resources, children's activity books designed for the general market often contain ideas that can be adapted very easily to illustrate a Christian story.

Bibles and Bible stories

Contemporary English Version of the Bible (HarperCollins, 2000)
New Revised Standard Version of the Bible (HarperCollins, 1989)
The Dramatised Bible (Marshall Pickering, 1989)
The Lion Children's Bible (Lion, 1981)
International Children's Bible (Nelson Word, 1983)
The Barnabas Children's Bible (Barnabas, 2007)
The Children's Illustrated Bible (Dorling Kindersley, 1994)
The Usborne Children's Bible (Usborne, 2000)
My Book of Bible Stories (Lion, 2002)
Stories Jesus Told, Nick Butterworth and Mick Inkpen (Marshall Pickering, 1996)

Christian resource books

Young Children and Worship, Sonya Stewart and Jerome Berryman (Westminster John Knox Press, 1989)
Theme Games, Lesley Pinchbeck (SU, 1993)
Theme Games 2, Lesley Pinchbeck (SU, 2002)
The 'E' Book: Essential prayers and activities for faith at home, Gill Ambrose (National Society/Church House Publishing, 2000)
101 Ideas for Creative Prayers, Judith Merrell (SU, 1995)